BOTH WRONG AND BAD

PREFERENCE BY RACE

CARL COHEN

outskirts
press

Table of Contents

PROLOGUE

Both Wrong and Bad: Why Race Preference is Unjust and Hurtful

Any act or policy that gives more to some persons or groups than others because of their color, or their national origin, or their ethnic identity is rightly called *race preference*. Such preference is now widely given by corporations in employment, by government agencies in contracting, and by universities in admission. Race preference, even when its aims are honorable, is *wrong*, unjust. It is also *bad*, damaging to the groups preferred and to the society as a whole.

The rightness of any act and the goodness of its result are commonly distinguished. We all know that an act that is right -- telling the truth, for example, -- may have very unfortunate consequences; and an act that is wrong -- say an unjustifiable accusation -- may produce a beneficial outcome.

Likewise, the wrongness of an act and the badness of its result must be distinguished. The moral quality of an act or policy is one thing, the worth of the consequences it yields is another. Acts we know to be wrong may have delightful results; acts having constructive intentions

... i ...

sometimes yield disastrous consequences. As we distinguish the right from the good, so also must we distinguish the wrong from the bad.

In passing judgement on race preference, therefore, we must inquire both into its moral quality and into the merit of its product. Giving advantage to members of some ethnic groups -- to white people because they are white or to black people because they are black -- would be wrong even if its consequences were good. Such preference is forbidden in America -- by the Constitution of the United States, and by Federal law. In ignoring those principles race preference is plainly wrong. But its moral wrongness is most evident in its violation of fundamental principles of fair treatment. Some hold that race preference, even if apparently unfair, is nevertheless justified by its important social objectives. The preferential pill may be bitter (they say) but we must swallow it because it is good for us. If indeed preference is wrong, it would be wrong even if it were good for us. But in fact it is *not* good for us. It hinders our efforts to heal racial hostilities; it corrupts the institutions in which it is practiced; especially the universities. Worst of all, it undermines the minorities it purports to assist. The wrongness of race preference is compounded by its badness.

All this will be explained in the pages that follow. The tension between the American ideal of equal treatment and our historical failure to realize that ideal is where we must begin. Our progress toward a society that is racially just has been painfully slow. One chapter in that progress has been the development of affirmative action, followed by the well-intended transformation of affirmative action into a form of race preference. From the beginning of our country the wound that has not healed has been *race preference*. Its cruel unfairness has been matched only by the terrible damage it has done. Race preference is as bad as it is wrong.

Part One:
Equality and Race Preference

Chapter 1:

Equality as an American Ideal

Chapter 2:

Affirmative Action

Chapter 3:

Race Preference: The Transformation of Affirmative Action

CHAPTER 1

Equality as an American Ideal

Human equality has been the first principle of the American republic since its founding. Among the truths held to be self-evident in the *Declaration of Independence* the very first is that "all men are created equal." We begin with this conviction because it is precisely the equality of citizens that *justifies* universal participation in community government. The equality to which we pledge our allegiance is the ground, the philosophical bedrock, of the democracy we profess.

American political practice long failed to respect that ideal in the concrete; in some ways we fail still. But our laws and institutions have grown steadily more enlightened; we have moved gradually, even if too slowly, toward the fuller realization of the moral ideal of equality.

Slavery made a mockery of that ideal. With the cruel history of black slavery fresh in mind, equality became a focus of Congressional concern in the years following the Civil War. The 13th Amendment to our Constitution, ratified in 1865, forbad slavery, but it barely dented the racism of the time. A few months later, in the Civil Rights Act of 1866, Congress declared that:

[A]ll ... citizens of the United States... of every race and color...
shall have the same right ... to full and equal benefit of all laws
and proceedings for the security of person and property... and
shall be subject to like punishment, pains, and penalties and to
none other.

Forceful language -- but the condition of former slaves did not rapidly
improve. Two years later this principle of universal equality was incorporated into the *Constitution of the United States*. The first Section of the
14th Amendment to our Constitution, adopted in 1868, reads in part:
"No State shall ... deny to any person within its jurisdiction the equal
protection of the laws."[1] The 15th Amendment to the Constitution,
specifically forbidding voting discrimination on grounds of race, followed shortly afterward, in 1870.

Thus embedded in the Constitution, the principle of human equality
was implemented legislatively in the Civil Rights Act of 1875, whose
language is, again, unambiguous and forceful:

[A]ll persons within the jurisdiction of the United States shall
be entitled to the full and equal enjoyment of the accommodation, advantages, facilities, and privileges of inns, public
conveyances on land and water, theaters, and other places of
public amusement; subject only to the conditions and limitations established by law, and applicable alike to citizens of every
race and color...

Earnestly proclaimed and honestly intended -- yet these declarations
of principle and law did not come close to ending racial oppression in
America. Discrimination against blacks and other minorities, flouting
the Constitution yet enforced by state governments, remained almost
universal until the middle of the twentieth century.

The invidious *segregation* of the races was the everyday instrument of
this discrimination. The U.S. Supreme Court decision in the infamous

case of *Plessy v. Ferguson,*[2] although affirming the formal ideal of equality, did not question the underlying belief that the equality of the races is consistent with their legally enforced separation. Another sixty years of racial oppression had been invited. The repudiation of that "separate but equal" doctrine did not come until 1954, when deliberate, state-sponsored segregation was held at last to be inconsistent with the equality guaranteed by the Constitution. In the most momentous decision of the twentieth century, the Supreme Court spoke with one voice:

> We conclude that in the field of public education the doctrine of 'separate but equal' has no place. Separate educational facilities are inherently unequal.[3]

The root of the evil of government policies based on race had been laid bare by the lone dissenter in *Plessy,* Justice John Harlan, before the 20th century began. He wrote:

> In respect of civil rights common to all citizens, the *Constitution of the United States,* does not, I think, permit any public authority to know the race of those entitled to be protected in the enjoyment of such rights. . . I deny that any legislative body or judicial tribunal may have regard to the race of citizens when the civil rights of those citizens are involved.[4]

Well over a century has passed since that was written. It is instructive to look back yet further. A decade after the Civil War had ended, during the Congressional debate over what was to become the Civil Rights Act of 1875, a black Representative from North Carolina, Richard Cain, put into words the simple vision of racial justice that a serious commitment to equality entails. On the floor of the Congress he said:

> All we ask is that you, the legislators of the nation, shall pass a law so strong and so powerful that no one shall be able to elude it and destroy our rights under the Constitution and

laws of our country. That is all we ask. . . . We do not want any discriminations. I do not ask any legislation for the colored people of this country that is not applied to the white people. All that we ask is equal laws, equal legislation, and equal rights throughout the length and breadth of this land.[5]

The reasonableness and cogency of his plea could not be denied. Imbued with that spirit precisely, the civil rights movement later became the nation's conscience. The demand for equality in practice is morally irresistible. Nothing less than genuinely equal treatment for all races, enforced by law, is tolerable in this country.

The ideal was far easier to express, however, than to achieve. To spur action guided by that ideal, to touch the moral nerve of the American public, heroes of the civil rights movement were obliged to defy discriminatory statutes, often at great personal risk, sometimes even at the cost of their lives. They were convinced, as we now earnestly sing, that the ideal of equal treatment for all must eventually overcome. With gathering momentum the United States turned away — reluctantly at first, but with gathering speed — from the long-ensconced patterns of racial oppression.

A full century after the close of the Civil War the great Civil Rights Act of 1964 was adopted.[6] This federal statute, in its many sections, makes discrimination *unlawful* when exercised by governments or employers in this country "against any individual . . . because of such individual's race, color, religion, sex, or national origin." On the day that Act was adopted, all 100 members of the United States Senate voting, it might have seemed that the law so long sought had at last been enacted, a law 'strong enough and powerful enough that no one shall be able to elude it.'"

The words of the Civil Rights Act of 1964 gave specificity and concreteness to the Constitutional guarantee of the "equal treatment of the laws." In employment, in education, in all spheres of public accommodation, there was to be from that time forward *no official favoritism for one race or ethnic group at the expense of others.* The intentions of the members of Congress in adopting this law were expressed clearly and emphatically. In extended debates on the floor of the Senate and the House during that summer of 1964 the comprehensive and unambiguous purpose of the legislators was again and again made explicit. Race preference was to be entirely eliminated. Attending carefully to the words they used, representatives and senators, one after the other, proclaimed in carefully chosen words that with the passage of this legislation all races in America were henceforth to be treated equally in the public sphere. The plain force of the language of the law was repeatedly emphasized. So clear was their meaning, they said on the floor of Congress, that the legal requirement of equal treatment could not thereafter be mistaken.

This Civil Rights Act of 1964, still very much the law of our nation, was politically momentous and also morally fine. In matters pertaining to race it marks the highest point reached in our national consciousness.[7]

End Notes -- Chapter I

[1] A more careful examination of this equal protection clause, as it bears upon race preference, appears below in Chapter 6.

[2] 163 U.S. 537 (1896). Citations of court decisions, of which there will be unavoidably many, have four parts: [1] the series of reports in which the decision is published. (U. S. Supreme Court decisions are published in (among others) *United States Reports,* abbreviated as U.S.), [2] preceded by the number of the volume in that series, and [3] followed by the page number in that volume, with [4] the year of the decision, in parentheses, concluding the citation. The citation in this footnote thus shows that the decision in the case of *Plessy v. Ferguson,* handed down in 1896, was published in volume 163 of *United States Reports,* beginning on p. 537.

[3] *Brown v. Board of Education,* 347 U.S. 483 (1954)

[4] 163 U.S. 537, at p. 555. Emphasis added.

[5] Richard H. Cain, cited by Frances F. Freeman, ed., in *The Black American Experience,* NY, Bantam Books, 1979, p. 116.

[6] It now appears in full, as amended, in Chapter 42 of the United States Codes.

[7] A more detailed examination of the language of the Civil Rights Act of 1964, and the debate over its enactment, appears below in Chapter 5.

CHAPTER 2

Affirmative Action

The unambiguous provisions of the Civil Rights Act of 1964 could not by themselves bring public racial discrimination to an end. In employment, in the admission of students to universities, in public accommodation, in the letting of government contracts, in housing rentals and sales, in the nooks and crannies of American life discriminatory practices had become embedded. Everyday procedures had to be reviewed and their discriminatory infections identified; a heightened sensitivity to racial unfairness was essential if that unfairness were to be effectively addressed. Detailed regulations were needed to cleanse institutions of their discriminatory -- often inadvertently discriminatory -- elements. Positive steps were needed to uproot the preferences long given to whites and to males.

President Lyndon Johnson's commitment to racial justice was whole-hearted. He had worked assiduously for the 1964 passage of the Civil Rights Act. In 1965 he issued Executive Order #11246, adding muscle to its provisions. Racial discrimination had come to infect federal employment, and also the work force of the private firms with which the federal government does business. President Johnson's Executive Order sought to combat the racism that had penetrated those workplace environments. It had these explicit objectives:

... to provide equal opportunity in federal employment for all persons, to prohibit discrimination in employment because of race, creed, color, or national origin, and to promote the full realization of equal opportunity through a positive, continuing program in each executive department or agency.[1]

This order initiated our national commitment to *affirmative* action — our determination to take positive steps to extirpate all preference by race. The term "affirmative action" had been used in an earlier order issued by President Kennedy,[2] and also (with the aim of eliminating discrimination against union members) in federal labor legislation in the 1930s.[3] But it was with the words and acts of Lyndon Johnson that affirmative action to promote racial equality began in earnest.

From that time forward -- Executive Order #11246 remains in effect -- every contractor dealing with the United States government has been obliged to agree as follows:

The contractor will not discriminate against any employee or applicant for employment because of race, creed, color, or national origin. The contractor will take *affirmative action* to ensure that applicants are employed, and that employees are treated during employment, *without regard to their race*, creed, color, or national origin.[4]

This enforceable assurance of *non-discrimination* extends to every aspect of employment: promotion, demotion, transfer, recruitment, termination, training, and rates of pay. Affirmative action was conceived as a sustained network of efforts — by the federal government in the first instance, and by all those who deal with it as well -- to insure that race, creed, color, and national origin were not to be the grounds of differential treatment. With respect to sex, those same assurances of non-discrimination were demanded two years later.[5]

Those wrongfully denied the equal treatment obliged by the Civil Rights Act came to the courts to be "made whole," to be compensated for their unjust injury. The language of the statute recognized the likely need for remedial relief, explicitly providing that, when some practice (e.g. in employment, or in college admissions) is found by a court to have been discriminatory, that court will have the authority to "order such affirmative action as may be appropriate." *Affirmative action* came to have the backing of the law.

What affirmative action *was* – as specified in the language of both the executive and legislative branches of our government -- was not originally in doubt. It was to be a variety of positive steps, designed appropriately in each context, to make concrete the ideal of equal protection under the law. By identifying discriminatory preferences long entrenched, eliminating them, and where feasible by redressing them, affirmative action became the banner of the *equality* of citizens of all races.

So conceived, affirmative action was morally right, as honorable as public policy can be. The ideal of equality had been formally recognized and protected by unambiguous federal statute in 1964. The realization of that ideal was now to be advanced by well-designed efforts. Affirmative action was to be the instrument with which we would expose and uproot the unequal treatment of racial groups, whether deliberate or inadvertent. Affirmative action deserved its good name. It spoke then, and it speaks now, to our condition.

End Notes -- Chapter 2

[1]   Executive Order No. 11246, 1965, Part I, Sec. 101.

[2]   Executive Order No. 10925, 1961.

[3]   National Labor Relations Act, 1935.

[4]   Executive Order No. 11246, Part 11, Sec. 202. Emphasis added.

[5]   Executive Order No. 113754, issued by President Lyndon Johnson in 1967.

CHAPTER 3

The Transformation of Affirmative Action

The Civil Rights Act of 1964 forbad race preference in American public life. It was designed to give teeth to the guarantee that the laws would be "applicable alike to citizens of every race and color." Less than seven years after its passage however, public and private bodies were giving outright preference by race in the name of "affirmative action." Affirmative action had been rapidly and dramatically transformed.

That transformation resulted in part from the fact that there are two competing visions of racial justice. The first is that of a society in which race has ceased to be an instrument for invidious classification, a society in which, as Justice Harlan had put it in *Plessy,* no public authority is permitted "to know the race" of those entitled to be protected. The second vision is that of a society in which the goods of social life are distributed evenly among all ethnic groups, a society in which racial imbalance has been overcome. The distinction of these two conceptions was not at first commonly noted, partly because it was widely supposed that, when the barriers created by racial segregation were at last torn down, balance in the distribution of social goods would quickly follow.

That did not happen. As I write, more than half a century after the enactment of the great Civil Rights Act, formal segregation in America is forbidden and despised. Many among us cannot even recall its ugly forms. But racial balance in a fully integrated society, balance in employment, integration in residential patterns, the approximately even distribution of wealth and education and other goods among our ethnic clusters, is very far from realization. This is due in part to the persistence of outright racism. In part also it is due to the fact that groups of human beings adopt different styles of life and share the drive to cluster with others like themselves. Although as a nation we have overcome much of the bigotry once rampant among us, we have been unable to transform our society into one that is fully integrated. Evil forces among us are not the chief reason for this. Social magnets arising naturally pull persons of similar cultural heritage together and reinforce patterns of racial difference. Cultural homogeneity does not appear to be feasible in the United States; many think it not at all desirable. *The New York Times* (in a report headed "The Unmet Promise of Equality", 1 March 2018) noted that in 2018 the percentage of schools segregated *de facto* (in which black students constitute 90 to 100 percent of the student body) in southern states *rose* from 24 in 1968 to 34 in 2011. In western states the rise of *de facto* segregation was from 26 to 34 percent; in northeastern states it was from 45 to 51 percent. There are formally de-segregated cities in America that are less fully integrated now, in the 21st century, than they were in 1964.[1] The fact that this reality has multiple causes, some evil and some not, has greatly complicated the history of affirmative action.

The unanimous Supreme Court order in *Brown* (in 1954) to desegregate the public schools had results far short of what had been hoped for. Many school boards, supported by their state governments, retained segregated schools, dual systems in violation of the law. Frustrated federal courts were repeatedly obliged to intervene, to oversee the schools, and then again to order -- sometimes in anger -- the desegregation that the Constitution requires.[2] The continuing obstinate refusal of some states to provide fully equal educational opportunities for those of all races could not be justified. What judges demanded, and the citizenry deserved, was a plan for school desegregation that promised to work, and (as one Court put it in a famous school case more than a decade after *Brown*) "promises realistically to work now."[3] We feel the frustration and share the indignation of that federal judge, and we applaud his vigor and sense of urgency.

State-supported segregation of the public schools did eventually come to an end. Federal courts used their powers to insure that pupils would be brought, by buses if that were the only way feasible, to schools affording equal opportunity. Federal marshals gave physical protection where it proved essential. The demand for equal treatment was reasonable and right; the outcome was to be school systems that were *unitary*. Every student in a public school district is *qualified* for equal treatment, and *entitled* to equal treatment. If school boards (or the states) failed to satisfy this entitlement they could be forced to obey. Some force did prove necessary, but eventually they did obey.

That demand for equality of outcome was extrapolated from the sphere of the public schools to the sphere of colleges, professional schools, and private employment. This extrapolation was mistaken. Where admission or appointment is competitive, the number of available slots being far too small to accommodate all applicants, an outcome in which success is enjoyed equally by all is not possible. The circumstances are not like those of the public schools. Not all who seek college admission, or well-paying jobs, are equally qualified for the prizes that are in limited supply. Where minority applicants are generally less well qualified, the demand for racial balance cannot be satisfied. Proportionality of outcome by race supposes an approximately equal possession of needed skills and attainments by race. But those qualifications were, and remain, far from proportionally distributed. No court orders or federal marshals can make them so.

Competition for the limited number of admission places, at the most prestigious colleges and professional schools, is intense. The proportion of minority applicants able to compete successfully for desired places has long been smaller than the proportion of those minorities in the population at large. It was not the invidious segregation of the races that made this so. By the late decades of the 20th century formal discrimination against minority applicants in higher education had ceased to be the rule. Universities have welcomed minority applicants, devised programs designed to encourage and support them, and sincerely promoted their success. Notwithstanding these efforts, racial proportionality, although a reasonable demand in public school systems, was an unrealistic expectation in professional schools, in laboratories, and in newsrooms. For many reasons, chiefly because of earlier educational deficiencies, the racial balance hoped for could not be soon achieved, even after discriminatory barriers had been torn down.

This reality was difficult to accept if one were convinced that desegregation would bring racial balance in its train. Desirable appointments in colleges and professional schools ought to be enjoyed proportionately by race, but they were not. How make them so? Affirmative action had been essential to erase the vestiges of segregation; all were agreed about that. Now, with formal segregation eliminated, the proportional results anticipated had not nearly been achieved. If such results were called for but had not been produced, this must be (it was reasoned) because the steps taken to promote them, although perhaps "affirmative," were not sufficiently vigorous.

Affirmative action applied in the spirit of Lyndon Johnson could not produce racial proportionality in the short term because it could not alter minority applicants in the ways needed to make them successful competitors, to make them qualified. Well then, came the response in effect, we need to take affirmative steps that are more penetrating. We need to change the systems of admission or employment so that minority applicants are qualified. Social justice, it was argued, requires that the proportional result be obtained; we must devise the machinery -- call it affirmative action -- that will move us toward that racial balance now.

We may be unable to change the applicants who apply, but we can change the standards for qualification. Changing those standards (the argument continued) is now essential. Our objective is achievable without delay if race be considered as one element of qualification. We must re-think the ways in which minority applicants are recruited and promoted. Principles governing the competition for places must be adjusted (it was argued), some of our earlier suppositions amended. Equal treatment does not yield the racially proportional results that are the hallmark of justice, so we must go beyond equal treatment. A racially balanced society is our rightful aim; we must not fear the social engineering required to achieve it.[4] Race-sensitive programs must be designed that will produce a racially balanced society. Such programs of social engineering, deliberate and resolute, took the good name of "affirmative action."

In only a few years affirmative action was thoroughly transformed. What could not be achieved through equal opportunity was indeed achieved when opportunity itself was reconsidered. To achieve the desired racial outcomes minority preference was given -- and is today still widely given -- in the competition for admission and employment. An honorable sense of moral urgency merged with unrealistic objectives. Institutional practices came to be driven by the conviction that social arrangements would be just only when racial balance had been achieved. Racial proportionality became the unspoken, and for many the unquestioned measure of success.

At first, modest preferences for minority applicants in closely competitive situations were thought to be all that would be needed. This proved mistaken. Plus factors at the margins were woefully insufficient.

Affirmative action was essential. This term, originally denoting programs that would eradicate preference by race, had its meaning inverted. In the name of techniques designed to uproot preference, preference was now introduced. Race preference was widely incorporated by institutions both public and private. In some contexts it became obligatory. Affirmative action was transformed into its opposite.

Cleansing institutions of the remnants of race discrimination is right. Redress for persons who have suffered known injuries because of their race is right. Designing procedures that are truly race-neutral is right. Those objectives are honorable, and affirmative action to advance them is not in question. At issue now is unequal treatment of the races in the name of equality. At issue now is preference given to persons because they are members of one or another racial group. At issue now is not affirmative action in its original sense, but in its inverted sense, preference by race.

Race preference, I now go on to show, is very wrong and very bad.

End Notes -- Chapter 3

[1] In Boston, to take one example, the number of white students in elementary public schools continues to decline, has dropped from 7,551 in 1990 to 4,431 in 2000, and now accounts for less than 14% of the elementary student body. And in some cities, Detroit for example, the percentage of black students in the public schools is higher than that in Boston. In 2014 *The Buffalo News* reported that 70% of that city's schools were once again segregated, a segregated school being defined as one in which 80% of the students were minorities, or were whites. Racial balance in metropolitan public schools in the near future is not probable. See "White Student Ratios Falling," *The Boston Globe*, 31 January 2002.

[2] There was much argument in the courts at that time, regarding the speed with which the achievement of the goals of *Brown I* was reasonably to be expected. In *Brown II* the Supreme Court had remanded that case, and other school segregation cases, to the lower courts with the instruction to "take such proceedings and enter such orders and decrees consistent with this opinion as are necessary and proper to admit to public schools on a racially nondiscriminatory basis *with all deliberate speed .. (Brown II*, p. 301, emphasis added.) But the meaning of the phrase "with all deliberate speed" also long remained in dispute.

[3] *Green v. School Board of New Kent County, NC,* 391 U.S. 430, at p. 439 (1968).

[4] A century before, in Germany, the overriding goal of national unification was believed by the Prussian authorities to require means that many thought to be unacceptable. But what is unacceptable? Bismarck is said to have responded: "Gangrene will not be cured with lavender water!" That was in 1870. In 2002 a leading organization committed to the continuation of race preferences in the United States calls itself BAMN — By Any Means Necessary.

Part Two:
Why Race Preference is Wrong

Chapter 4:
Race Preference is Morally Wrong

Chapter 5:
Race Preference is Against the Law

Chapter 6:
Race Preference Violates the U.S. Constitution

CHAPTER 4

Race Preference Is
Morally Wrong

(1) The Principle of Equality

That *equals should be treated equally* is a fundamental principle of morality. Race preference is morally wrong because it violates this principle.

But who are equals?[1] Identical treatment for everyone in all matters is certainly not just. Citizens have privileges that non-citizens do not have; employers have responsibilities that employees do not have; higher taxes may be rightly imposed upon those with higher incomes; the right to vote is withheld from the very young. Groups of persons may deserve different treatment because they are different in critical respects. But what respects are critical? The elderly and the disabled have special needs that justify community concern. This much is clear: unequal treatment by the state demands explanation. What justifies the state in doing for some preferred group what it does not do for others?

When preference for some group is agreed upon in principle we may yet disagree about what precisely differentiates the class to be advantaged.

Physical disabilities may justify special accommodation, while the kinds of disabilities that should qualify for that accommodation remain in dispute. If tuition at a state university is lower for residents than for non-residents, the criteria for residency must be plainly set forth. Only adults may vote, of course -- but what is the age of adulthood? Higher taxes for the wealthy, yes -- but how are graduated tax schedules to be designed? The principle of equality does not require that all be treated identically, but when some receive a public benefit that others do not, that preference will be unfair unless the advantages given can be justified by some feature of the group preferred. Unequal treatment by the state requires defense.

Some defenses are flatly unacceptable. Some group characteristics are simply not relevant to the preference given. Ancestry we reject. Better treatment for Americans of Irish descent than for those of Polish descent is wrong; we have no doubt about that. Sex we reject. Privileges to which men are entitled cannot be denied to women. Religion we reject. Opportunities open to Catholics must be open to Jews. Color we reject. When the state favors white skin over black skin -- a practice common for centuries -- we are now outraged. Such categories cannot determine desert. This matter is settled. In dealings with the state, persons *may not* be preferred because of their race, or color, or religion, or sex, or national origin.

Bigots, of course, will draw distinctions by race (or nationality, etc.) in their private lives. But private opinions, however detestable, are not public business. The matter is very different when the body politic frames the rules. With respect to the civil rights that citizens of the United States enjoy, bigotry is forbidden. Persons of all colors, religions, and origins are equals with respect to their rights, equals in the eyes of the law. And equals must be treated equally. Race and nationality simply cannot serve, in our country, as the justification for unequal treatment.

This we do not learn from any book or document. It is not true because it is expressed in the *Declaration of Independence*, or laid down in *The Constitution of the United States*. On the contrary, the principles flowing from human equality are found in those great documents *because* they are true. That "all men are created equal" is one way, perhaps the most famous way, of expressing the central moral truth involved. That the "equal protection of the laws," is not to be denied to any person by any state (as the Fourteenth Amendment to our Constitution provides) is one way of giving that moral truth political teeth. Our great documents *recognize* and *realize* moral principles grasped by persons everywhere: All the members of humankind are equally ends in themselves, all have equal *dignity* -- and therefore all are entitled to equal respect from the community and its laws.

John Dewey, rightly thought of as the philosopher of democracy, put it this way:

> "Equality does not mean mathematical equivalence. It means rather the inapplicability of considerations of. . . superior and inferior. It means that no matter how great the quantitative differences of ability, strength, position, wealth, such differences are negligible in comparison with something else — the fact of individuality, the manifestation of something irreplaceable. . . . It implies, so to speak, a metaphysical mathematics of the incommensurable in which each speaks for itself and demands consideration on its own behalf."[2]

This recognition of the ultimate equality and fellowship of humans with one another is taught by great thinkers in every culture — by Buddha, and St. Francis, and Walt Whitman. At bottom we all recognize, as the political philosopher Walter Lippmann wrote:

> "a spiritual reality behind and independent of the visible character and behavior of a man. . . . We know, each of us, in a way too certain for doubting, that, after all the weighing and

comparing and judging of us is done, there is something left over which is the heart of the matter."[3]

This is the moral standard against which race preference must be judged. The principle of equality certainly entails at least this: it is wrong, always and everywhere, to give special advantages to any group simply on the basis of physical characteristics that have no relevance to the award given or to the burden imposed. To give or to take on the basis skin color is manifestly unfair.

The most gruesome chapters in human history — the abomination of black slavery, the wholesale slaughter of the Jews — remind us that *racial* categories must never be allowed to serve as the foundation for official differentiation. Nations in which racial distinctions were once embedded in public law are forever shamed. Our own history is by such racism ineradicably stained. The lesson is this: Never again. Never, *ever* again.

What is today loosely called "affirmative action" is seriously problematic because it fails to respect that lesson. It uses categories that *must not* be used to distinguish among persons with respect to their entitlements in the community. Blacks and whites are equals, as blondes and brunettes are equals, as Catholics and Jews are equals, as Americans of every ancestry are equal. No matter who the beneficiaries may be or who the victims, preference on the basis of race is morally wrong. It was wrong in the distant past and in the recent past; it is wrong now, and it will always be wrong. Race preference violates the principle of human equality.

(2) Race Preference Cannot Be Justified as Compensatory

Millions of persons have been injured because of their race, damaged or deprived because they were black or brown. Do they not deserve some redress? They do, of course. But it is the *injury* they suffered for which compensation ought be given in such cases, not the color of the skin of those injured.

Some will argue that it is precisely the harms so long inflicted on racial minorities that justify the special consideration of those racial groups. Bearing the cruel past in mind, they contend that deliberate preference for racial groups formerly oppressed is the way we reverse historical injustice, and thereby make fair what might seem to be unfair. African Americans, Native Americans, Hispanics, and other minorities have for so many generations been the victims of outrageous discrimination that the sum of it is incalculable. Explicit preference to these minorities today compensates, in part, for injuries most certainly done. Historical wrongs cannot be undone, but (they contend) we can take some steps toward the restoration of moral balance.

At this point in our history, those advocates continue, equal treatment is in fact not just. Minorities have been so long shackled by discriminatory laws and economic deprivation that it is not fair to oblige them to compete now against a majority never burdened in that way. The visible burdens have been removed, but not the residual impact of their long imposition. We must *level the playing field* in the competition for employment, university admission, and other goods. Only explicit race preference can do this; therefore explicit race preference is just.

This is the argument in support of race preference upon which most of its contemporary advocates chiefly rely. The argument is grounded upon the demand for *compensation*, for redress. It seeks to turn the tables in the interests of justice. White males, so long the beneficiaries of preference, are now rightly obliged to give preference to others. Past oppression, say the current advocates of compensatory racial preference, must be paid for. Is turnabout not fair play?

No, not when the instrument turned is itself essentially unjust. The compensatory argument seems plausible, but it is mistaken. Preference *by* race cannot serve as just compensation for earlier wrongs done because of race. It cannot do so because race is a crude and morally irrelevant standard. The accidents of birth -- color, national origin, and the like -- have no moral weight. The historical injustices we now seek to redress were themselves a product of moral blindness; they were inflicted because burdens and benefits were awarded on grounds irrelevant to what was deserved. Blacks and browns were not injured by *being* black or brown. They were injured by treatment unfairly *based* upon their being black or brown. The redress deserved is redress that goes to *them*, to those injured, in the light of the injuries they suffered. Many are long dead and can never be compensated. Those ancient injuries are not remedied by bestowing benefits now upon persons who happen to belong to the ethnic group of those injured.

Using race to award benefits now does injustice in the very same way injustice was earlier done, by giving moral weight to skin color in itself. The unfair use of racial classifications is no less unfair when directed at whites now than it was when directed at blacks then. A wrong is not redressed when the same wrong is done to others.

Moreover, by devising new varieties of race preference we give legitimacy to the consideration of race, reinforcing the very injustice we seek to eradicate. We compound injustice with injustice, again embedding racial categories in public policy and law.

The moral blindness of race preference is exhibited from both sides: the *wrong people benefit,* and *the wrong people pay the price of that benefit.*

Consider who benefits. Race preference rewards some persons who deserve no reward at all, and is thus *over* inclusive. Systems are designed to give special consideration to all those having some physical or genetic feature, all those who are black, or female, or of some specified national origin. Hispanics, for example, receive the advantage because they have parents or grandparents of certain national origins. But have all those of Hispanic origin been wrongly injured? Do all those of that (or of any) single national origin deserve compensation now for earlier injuries? Surely not. Many Hispanics have been discriminated against in our country, to be sure. But it is also true that many of Hispanic ancestry now enjoy and have long have enjoyed circumstances as decent and as well-protected as Americans of all other ethnicities. The same is true of African-Americans, some of whom are impoverished and some of whom are rich and powerful. Benefits distributed on the basis of ethnic membership assume that the damage suffered by some was suffered by all -- an assumption that we know to be false.

The falsehood of that assumption of universal injustice cannot be recognized and acted upon where race rules. The University of Texas (for example) long gave preference to all blacks seeking admission, contending that they were in this way giving remedy for the deprivations suffered by black children in the Texas public schools. Some of the very finest public school students (and public school teachers) in Texas are black, but race preference cannot recognize that, cannot attend to morally significant differences. Blackness, in itself, became the ground of race preference in Texas, so the finest black students graduating from Texas public schools received preference in university admission along with every other applicant whose skin was the same color. Applicants to the University of Texas who happened to be black were given preference even if they had not attended Texas public schools at all. It was their blackness that counted. Graduates of private schools in Dallas or Houston, if they were black, received admission preference as compensatory relief. Applicants might have come from any other state, attended public or private schools of any description -- but if they were black they were given preference at the University of Texas. Even those not schooled in the United States, graduates of schools in France or in India, were preferred because their skin was the right color. Preference in Texas was by color. Blind to moral considerations, color was all that was needed to insure special treatment there. The compensatory defense of preferential admissions, presented by the University of Texas in lengthy Federal litigation, was in the end rejected categorically by the U.S. Court of Appeals.[4]

Over-inclusiveness is unavoidable when racial categories are used, because those categories are too blunt to do justice. "Set-asides" for minority contractors illustrate the same crudity. To compensate for past discrimination against minority contractors in the city of Richmond, Virginia, the city council reserved 30% of all city contracts for minority-owned firms. Minority contractors who had previously done business in Richmond were few, their portion of city contracts had indeed been small. The preference given as compensatory, however, was awarded not only to Richmond firms that earlier suffered unfairly, but to every firm, wherever based, whose owners happened to be in one of certain specified racial categories, including Native Americans, Eskimos, and Aleuts. Discriminatory injustices against Eskimos and Aleuts in Richmond had surely been rare, but the compensatory instrument did not attend to that. The 30% set aside was a quantity of business impossible for the existing minority contractors of Richmond to cope with, so the statute obliged the award of compensatory benefits to minority contractors who had never suffered injustice in Richmond or anywhere -- and even to minority contractors based far beyond Virginia, who, if they had suffered at all, certainly had not been victims of any discrimination by the City of Richmond. Over-inclusive to the point of absurdity? Yes. But similar set-aside programs by race pervade city and state governments in America still, and our Federal government as well. Such preferences intensify the moral consequences of race, indirectly confirming the legitimacy of the very instrument of classification that we find repugnant.

Race preference is morally defective also in being *under* inclusive; it fails to reward many who deserve compensation. For what injuries might redress be deserved? Inadequate education perhaps: teachers poorly qualified, books in short supply, buildings vermin-infested and deteriorating, schools rotten all around. High school graduates who come to the verge of college admission having suffered handicaps like these may indeed deserve to have their past performance evaluated in the light of such deprivations. They may be worthy of special consideration -- consideration given not because of the color of their skins, but because of what they suffered and accomplished. Whatever compensatory relief we think the students of such inferior schools deserve is deserved by all such students, of whatever skin color.

Race preference is thus faulty in what it does not do, as well as in what it does. Blinded by race it cannot see what may truly justify special regard. It is not only blacks and Hispanics who have been burdened by bad schools, or undermined by poverty, or wounded by malfunctioning families. But those of some colors, however much they also may have been unfairly injured or deprived, get no support from what is called affirmative action. They are simply left out.

Also left out are those blacks (and other minorities) who were so seriously damaged by educational deprivation that they could not even enter the competition slots in professional schools, or for training programs, and therefore could not benefit from the race preferences now commonly given. So those most in need of help usually get none, and those equally entitled to help whose skins are the wrong color receive no affirmative consideration.

As a community response to social and economic adversity what we give must be given to persons without regard their race or sex or national origin. Because it is the injury and not the ethnicity for which relief may be in order, relief cannot be justly restricted to ethnic minorities. For any injury or deprivation that justifies compensatory redress, whites as well as blacks who have suffered it will be entitled to the same redress. Looking through racial lenses this truth cannot be seen.

In a just system remedies should be designed to compensate most those who were injured most, and to compensate least, or not at all, those who were injured least, or not at all. Therefore a sensitive regard for the nature of the injury suffered, and the degree of suffering, are critical in giving redress. However difficult it is to estimate the injury earlier suffered, naked race preference must fail because, by hypothesis, it does not regard variety or degree. How severely injured are those who have completed undergraduate studies and are competing for admission to professional schools? The daughter of a black physician who graduates from a fine college may be entitled to no preferential consideration in a competitive admissions system simply because she is black, but she will receive it. The principal beneficiaries of affirmative action in law schools and medical schools are the children of upper middle-class minority families; they are the minority applicants most likely to be in a position to apply to such schools. Those whose personal histories of deprivation may in truth entitle them to some special consideration are rarely in a position even to hope for preference in such contexts. One of the great ironies of affirmative action is that those among minority groups receiving its preferences are precisely those least likely to deserve them.

Obtuseness is encouraged when the success of affirmative action is determined by counting racial numbers. The implicit premise is that in the absence of oppressive mistreatment, the distribution of ethnic groups in educational and employment categories would be proportional to their percentage in the population at large. Supposing this, universities and private firms establish racial goals for minority admission and employment that roughly mirror the ethnic profile of the larger community. Those numerical targets are not commonly attainable. But the political pressure upon administrators to approach these goals is nevertheless intense; their jobs may depend on the racial numbers they report. In the law schools, for example, the question of whether those receiving favor truly deserve those special benefits is not even asked. The compensatory arguments that gave birth to the preferences are quite forgotten in the press for minority numbers. Our immediate concern, say the law school deans, is our student profile; we must have more black faces. In the world of professional employment also, numbers rule. An attorney defending the practice of laying off white teachers with high seniority to protect the jobs of black teachers with much lower seniority was asked by a Justice of the U.S. Supreme Court *why* the employment preference in question had been given. His answer was blunt but honest: "We want them there."[5] "Them" in such contexts refers to people having the color preferred; it mattered not at all to that school board that those persons had no claim whatever for compensatory relief. At the University of Michigan, where highly qualified majority applicants were rejected while minimally qualified minority applicants were accepted in their place, questions by admissions officers about the degree of injury suffered by those minority applicants were not asked; whether any discriminatory injury had been suffered was not their chief concern. They had racial balancing goals to meet.

What the University of Michigan did by formal rule. many other colleges and universities still do informally. Candor is rare in the world of college admissions. It is easy to see, and painful to note, that race preference commonly results in the enrollment of students who are deemed "qualified" only by stretching the concept of qualification to the point of duplicity. Standards in the appointment of faculty are also eroded. Affirmative action hiring goals result in the appointment of faculty who would not have been hired but for their race. Those favored include many who have been deprived of nothing, and were never injured because of their race.

In sum, race preference gives to those who don't deserve, and doesn't give to those who do. It awards more to those who deserve less, and less to those who deserve more. These failings are inescapable because the preferences in question are grounded not in earlier injury but in physical characteristics that cannot serve as just grounds for advantage or disadvantage. Whatever is owed persons because of injuries they suffered is owed them without any regard to their ethnicity. Many who may now deserve remedy for past abuse are not minority group members; many who are minority group members deserve no remedy. Preference awarded only to persons in certain racial categories, and to all in those categories whatever their actual desert, invariably overrides the moral considerations that are genuinely relevant, and cannot be rightly justified as compensatory.

(3) Race Preference Imposes Unfair Penalties Upon Those Not Preferred

Not only the benefits, but also the burdens imposed by race-based preferences are distributed unfairly. By attending chiefly to skin color, racial instruments impose penalties upon those (of the non-favored color) who deserve no penalty at all, persons entirely innocent of the earlier wrong for which the preference is allegedly given.

Consider the circumstances of those not preferred. In the vast majority of cases it is false to suppose that they are in any way responsible for the injuries of those now preferred, or of persons in the same racial category as those now preferred. A race-based system of penalty and reward is morally cockeyed.

In a setting in which applicants compete for goods in short supply (say, admission to a law school), advantages given to some must be paid for by disadvantages borne by others. This is a truth of logic that cannot be escaped. In those settings what is given to some must be taken from others. When some are advantaged because of their color or sex, others must be disadvantaged because of their color or sex. There is no ethnic preference that can be "benign."

Advocates of preference scoff at the alleged burden, contending that the impact of race preference on the majority is insignificant. The number of white job applicants, or white university applicants is huge, while the number of minority applicants given preference is small. So if those preferences impose a burden, the advocates contend, it is at worst a trivial burden because of the great number over whom that burden is distributed. The complaint about unfairness, the advocates conclude, thus makes a mountain of a molehill. Preferences given to minority applicants are (it is argued) so greatly diluted by the size of the majority that their consequences are barely detectable.

This argument is deceptive, its conclusion is false. Only some in the majority are directly affected, of course, and after preferences are given we cannot know who among those rejected would have been appointed or admitted if that preferential system had not been in place. But it does not follow that the burden of preference is insignificant. The full price must be paid. Some individual members of the majority must have been displaced, and upon them the burden is as heavy as it is unfair. Injustice is not trivial because we do not know the names of its victims.

Do this thought experiment: Suppose that you are the admissions officer of a fine law school. With due diligence you select those to be admitted by applying (at the direction of the governing faculty) only the criteria for admission appropriate for a law school: earlier academic performance, character, promise, related intellectual attainments, recommendations, performance on admissions examinations, and so on. Suppose, in a given year, that you avoid all racial classifications in weighing applicants, giving no preference for ethnic status or any other suspect classification. Some 400 persons are to be sent letters of acceptance. You write down each of their names in one long list, starting at the top with those whose acceptance was clear and uncontroversial, continuing with the names of less impressive applicants, completing the list with the names of those applicants who, although succeeding, barely made it above the cut-off line. There must have been a cut-off line because you considered many thousands of applicants, and the great majority of them had to have been rejected.[6]

Now suppose that you construct the list of accepted applicants a second time -- this time weighing also the preferences given to applicants of certain races actually employed at your law school. Again you write down the names of all those accepted in a long column. The two lists you have prepared will not be identical, of course, for if they were race would not have entered the process in the second listing, as we know that it did. Therefore there will be names on the second list that did not appear on the first -- the names of applicants who received special consideration because of their race. We will be happy for them. But there will also be -- there must also be -- some names on the first list that do not appear on the second. These are the persons who pay the price of the race preferences given on the second list. The applicants thus eliminated do not pay the price just a wee bit. There is no dilution of burden for them; they lose 100% of their erstwhile listing because they are not to be admitted. They are rejected, although by hypothesis they would have been admitted had there been no racial considerations introduced. With race weighed, some people must lose out in the competition who would not have lost out if race were not weighed. Those losers pay the full penalty of preference.

It may be a heavy penalty. Applicants who would otherwise have gotten the job don't get it; employees who might have been promoted don't get promoted. Those who might have been admitted to a college or professional school but are rejected because of their race and must go elsewhere, or perhaps go nowhere. The majority applicants who are squeezed out in this process are often the first members of their family pulling their way into the middle class. Upon them, not the established rich, the burden of preference is imposed..

Those who have been so displaced may suspect but cannot know that they are the ones paying this price. That first list constructed hypothetically in our thought experiment never gets compiled in fact. The names on it are never known, so the names of those deleted from it cannot be known when the second list takes its place. But there *is* such a first list. That is, there is a set of persons who would have been accepted had race not been weighed, and the set on the second list does take its place. The fact that we cannot name the persons squeezed out does not make the squeezing less unfair.

Of those many applicants who, with good reasons, believed their chances of admission or appointment were excellent, each is likely to infer, when rejected, that among the names squeezed out by race was hers or his. If only their skin color had been different, they may infer, the outcome would have been very different. The inference is not foolish. Some people do not get what they would have gotten if their color had not been held against them. This is seriously unjust. It is an unavoidable consequence of race preference.

The underlying problem is everywhere the same: in deciding upon what is to be given by way of redress for injury the appropriate considerations are the nature and degree of the injury itself, not the race or national origin of potential beneficiaries. When preference is given to some because of their race, some who do deserve redress do not receive it (either because they had been too greatly damaged to compete, or because they happen not to be members of the favored categories), while many who are members of the favored categories are owed nothing in the way of redress. Those who bear the burden of the preferential award are likely to be innocent, bearing no responsibility for injuries earlier done to the ethnic group preferred. Benefits and burdens both become a function of race, which ought not to have entered the arena. President John Kennedy said: "Race has no place in American life."

Race preference is plainly unsuited to achieve the compensatory objective commonly offered in its defense. It is morally wrong.

(4) Race Preference Cannot Be Justified by the Quest for Diversity

Diversity is worthy of pursuit. In universities especially, and wherever information is conveyed, as in journalism and publishing, intellectual diversity is especially important. Among teachers, students, reporters, and the like, a variety of perspectives, and a range of opinions, even conflicting opinions, is healthy. Differing styles of life contribute to the richness of our social world. But the usefulness of diversity, and the pride we take in it, does not make it a compelling moral consideration. The merits of diversity are often exaggerated, but even when they are not its benefits cannot override our obligation to deal with people of all races as equals.

As now used in this context, the term "diversity" does not mean variety of viewpoint and opinion; it means variety among the races in their proper proportions. Universities that might enrich their intellectual diversity do not much concern themselves with that objective. Diversity in political views, diversity in religions, diversity in lifestyles, diversity along many other dimensions that can provide intellectual enrichment is commonly ignored.[7] The only "diversity" that serves to justify preference is racial diversity. The standard by which it is decided whether diversity has been adequately achieved is the approximation of those in the several racial groups to the proportion of those minorities in the population at large. "Diversity" has become a euphemism for race proportionality. To force race proportionality forthrightly would require quotas that are highly objectionable and even unlawful, so the goal put forward is a race-neutral characteristic with wide appeal.

Even when the quest for diversity is undertaken in the most honorable sense it cannot justify an unfair distribution of goods. The benefits of a sought-after racial distribution cannot outweigh moral principles requiring fair treatment. Do this thought experiment: Suppose we are confronted with strong evidence that *segregated* classrooms improve learning and teaching. Suppose the data in support of segregation were very impressive, more impressive than the data offered in support of ethnic diversity. Would we think that such evidence (supposing it valid) constituted a justification for the deliberate racial segregation of our schools or classrooms? Of course we would not. We condemn racial discrimination authorized by the state. Whatever the evidence may show, racial discrimination is wrong, unacceptable. Advantages that may flow from it cannot not begin to justify a policy that is intrinsically unjust. The praises of diversity as an instrument of education are often overblown; that racial diversity has any measurable impact upon the quality of learning in a university is in serious doubt.[8] But even if those claims of benefit had substantial merit, in a moral community they would carry little weight. Racial discrimination imposed by the state is despicable, we know. Whichever race is favored by some discriminatory policy, the policy itself is morally intolerable; no studies aiming to persuade us of its educative benefits can make it acceptable.

(5) Outreach as Affirmative Action

To overcome the racism that has long pervaded American society we have a duty to insure that persons of all races and ethnicities have genuine and equal opportunities in all spheres of social life. Where previously invidious exclusion had been the rule, inclusion must now replace it. Deliberate efforts to accomplish this is a duty deserving emphasis. However, it cannot justify race preference.

Truly equal opportunity requires a flow of information not restricted to the members of the establishment. In public settings, systems that rely on an inner network of friends or acquaintances are unjust. They are also counterproductive because they result in the loss of the contributions of those who come from outside the inner circle. Reaching out to the larger community in announcing opportunities, in offering scholarships, in posting available jobs, and so on, is morally right.

Qualified members of all ethnicities, of both sexes, are entitled to the educational and employment opportunities that white males have traditionally enjoyed. Where the availability of jobs and educational opportunities has long favored some and disfavored others, honest outreach, favoring none, may overcome those barriers. Acting vigorously to extend inclusiveness, advertising with the deliberate aim of reaching groups beyond those already well represented, is fully justifiable *affirmative action* in the original and honorable sense of that much abused term. To it we may all subscribe.

In summary: Race preference conflicts with the principle of equality that every decent society ought to respect. Race preference cannot be justified as a compensatory device. It cannot be justified by the quest for diversity. It cannot be justified by the call for outreach. It is morally wrong.

End Notes -- Chapter 4

[1]   Aristotle wrote:"All men admit ... that equals ought to receive equally. But there still remains a question: equal treatment for equality or inequality of what?" *Politics*, Book III, chapter 12.

[2]   *Characters and Events*, Vol. II, 1929, p. 854.

[3]   *Men of Destiny*. 1927, p. 50.

[4]   See: Thomas E. Wood and Malcolm J. Sherman, "Race and Higher Education," National Association of Scholars, available online at *www.nas.org*.

CHAPTER 5

Race Preference Breaks the Law

(1) The Civil Rights Act of 1964

Deliberate racial discrimination is wrong because it violates the Civil Rights Act of 1964. That Act prohibits racial discrimination in a variety of public settings. It is constituted by a large set of laws, grouped into parts called Titles, each of which is a family of prohibitions bearing upon some sphere of social life. References to the Act are made by specifying, by number, the Title that governs in the matter at hand.[1]

Thus, as examples: Discrimination in places of public accommodation is forbidden by Title III. Title VI deals with the denial of benefits by race or national origin in any institution receiving federal financial assistance, which includes all public schools and most universities. Title VII forbids discriminatory employment practices, in both the public and the private sector. (It is complemented by Executive Orders 11246 (1965) and Executive Order 11375 (1967) which lay down rules that govern public contractors, and speak to them; they command that federal employment be "without discrimination because of race, color, religion, or national origin.") Title IX forbids discrimination on the basis of sex.

The wording of this great set of laws plainly shows that the several Titles, and Sections, were directed not only to employers and administrators but to government agencies and courts whose duty it would be to enforce the Act. Thus for example we find the following passage in Title VII:

> Nothing contained in this subchapter shall be interpreted to require any employer, employment agency, labor organization, or joint labor-management committee subject to this subchapter to grant preferential treatment to any individual or to any group because of the race, color, religion, sex, or national origin of such individual or group on account of an imbalance which may exist with respect to the total number or percentage of persons of any race, color, religion, sex, or national origin employed by an employer, referred or classified by any employment agency or labor organization, or admitted to, or employed in, any apprenticeship or other training program, in comparison with the total number of persons of such race, color, religion, sex or national origin in any community, State, section, or other area, on in the available workforce in any community, State, section, or other area.[2]

This anti-discriminatory theme, set forth with lucidity and with detailed care in phrasing, is manifest throughout the Sections and Titles of the Civil Rights Act of 1964. One Justice of the Supreme Court, calling attention years later to the great clarity of its language, commends this Act as "a model of statutory draftsmanship."[3] No person who understands English can doubt that the object of this Civil Rights Act was, and is, to make unlawful (in those spheres to which the law expressly applies) all discrimination on the basis of race, color, religion, sex, or national origin.

Affirmative action programs in education, government, and industry are not exempt. Race preference given under such programs is a violation of law. One need not be a scholar or a judge to see this; the words of the statute can hardly be misunderstood. Employers, university administrators, and all others who discriminate, who give special favor to some races over others, break the law.

Race preference was squarely addressed in 1978 by the Supreme Court of the United States in a landmark case, *Regents of the University of California v. Alan Bakke.*[4] The racially preferential admissions system of that University was struck down, and Mr. Bakke ordered admitted. Justice Stevens, joined in his concurring opinion by three other Supreme Court Justices, relied specifically and solely upon the language of Title VI:

> No person in the United States shall, on the ground of race, color, or national origin, be excluded from participation in, be denied the benefits of, or be subjected to discrimination under any program or activity receiving Federal financial assistance.[5]

Having noted that the University of California acknowledges that it receives federal financial assistance, he wrote: "The plain language of the statute therefore requires, "that the judgment of the Supreme Court of California striking down admissions preferences at the University of California be affirmed and Bakke admitted." Justice Stevens continued:

> Nothing in the legislative history justifies the conclusion that the broad language of Section 601 should not be given its natural meaning. We are dealing with a distinct statutory prohibition. . . . In unmistakable terms the Act prohibits the exclusion of individuals from federally funded programs because of their race. As succinctly phrased during the Senate debate, under Title VI it is not "permissible to say 'yes' to one person but to say 'no' to another person, only because of the color of his skin.". . . The University's special admissions program violated Title VI of the Civil Rights Act of 1964 by excluding Bakke from the medical school because of his race.[6]

Race preference in institutions receiving federal assistance is impermissible *as a matter of federal law* in the United States of America. No qualifications, no conditions, no uncertainties have place here: Race preference breaks the law.

(2) Evading the Civil Rights Act

If the law be so clear, how has it been possible to maintain racially preferential programs that blatantly violate it? Evasion has most often been protected by subterfuge.

Racially discriminatory conduct is often disguised so as to make it appear that the law is being obeyed. Deception has been common. Affirmative action programs are described as designed to support "disadvantaged" persons, where the only disadvantaged persons considered in some institutions are members of ethnic minorities for whom preference is intended. The implicit premise relied upon is that all members of certain minorities are necessarily disadvantaged; this conviction is used to justify race preference while describing that preference as support for the disadvantaged.

Compensation for social or economic disadvantage certainly does not violate the Civil Rights Act. But all disadvantaged persons are not members of some ethnic minority, nor are all members of the often-protected minorities disadvantaged. Therefore, when preferences are awarded in fact on the basis of race, but are described to the public as no more than efforts to overcome social or economic disadvantage, we are confronting cheats. Cheating of this kind has been widely practiced.

Three examples:

(1) The California court that first struck down the preferential admissions program of the Davis Medical School at the University of

California (in *Regents v. Bakke*) noted that the program had been carefully described by the University in its letters to applicants as applying to "applications from economically and/or educationally disadvantaged backgrounds." The court found, however, that it was in fact a system of preference based only on ethnic membership, since no applicants other than those from approved "affirmative action categories" had *ever* been admitted under the special admissions program. The Supreme Court of California, reviewing the matter, agreed.[7] The Medical School had deliberately sought to make it appear that its standards were race-neutral although its conduct made it evident that this was knowing subterfuge. No one having an opportunity to examine the data would be fooled — but those data were brought to light only by litigation. The University was sharply scolded for its deliberate obfuscation. Chastened, the University of California ceased to argue that its program was not racially preferential.

(2) At the University of Michigan a quarter of a century later, after a lengthy trial, a federal judge found that the published account of the admissions program at its law school was deceptive. The law school had claimed that it sought only to enroll a "critical mass" of minority students; the judge held that, in fact, the system in use there was "indistinguishable from a quota system." Descriptions of race preference deliberately designed to mislead remain common. Obfuscation to evade the law is widely practiced at our colleges and universities.

(3) Not in universities only is the term "disadvantaged" used when "minority" is the real meaning. A federal statute provides that cash bonuses are to be paid to firms contracting with the U.S. Government if their sub-contractors are minority owned. This is plainly race preference. The language of the regulations applied, however, is framed not in terms of "minority" ownership but in terms of "disadvantaged" ownership. The bonus payments are to be made to encourage *"disadvantaged business enterprises"* -- DBEs, as they have come to be known. That would appear innocent — but the definitions used in the statute

ensure that all sub-contractors not members of the white majority are automatically to be treated as "disadvantaged business enterprises."[8] And so it goes.

Names are used for subterfuge. The names given to affirmative action programs at colleges and universities are often designed to hide their racial character and preferential purpose. At the University of Michigan admissions preference was called "The Michigan Mandate." At Pennsylvania Military College preferentially admitted students who did not satisfy ordinary admission standards were enrolled in "Project Prepare." But only persons of certain colors were thus prepared.

Supreme Court Justice Lewis Powell expressed his view, in the 1978 *Bakke* decision that "diversity," may be a justification for the consideration of race in college admissions.[9] That word gave promise as a shield in litigation. "Diversity" became in consequence a widely used code word designating the goal of racial proportionality where it is thought not prudent to state that objective candidly. The quest for "diversity" now commonly *means* the quest for increased minority participation. Other common code words -- "multi-culturalism" and "cultural pluralism" -- have similar equivocating functions.

The truth does not fare well in public reports about these matters. Caught between the political need to advance racial balance (to "promote diversity") on the one hand, and the legal prohibition of race discrimination on the other hand, administrators sometimes lie. To admit publicly that they give naked preference by race would be professionally unacceptable, yet the "improvement" of the minority percentages (in enrollment or employment) has become a professional necessity. Professional success is not possible, in many contexts, unless race preference be given.

Even in such contexts outright lying is risky. So it is often hidden by doublespeak in which a message that cannot be delivered forthrightly is conveyed backhandedly. From the "Affirmative Employment Division" of the U.S. Air Force Academy an applicant receives this instruction:

> The Federal Government is an equal opportunity employer and in support of that effort we ask that you voluntarily complete the Standard Form 181, "Race and National Origin Identification."[10]

Racial discrimination is against the law, says this government employer, and we comply with the law -- but we prefer minorities. Are you one? The tell-tale phrase that signals race preference by employers is the common self-description in help-wanted advertisements, an "affirmative action /equal opportunity employer." Orwell would chuckle.

The sham is universally recognized, but almost everyone is made complicit and so almost everyone winks. Wrongdoing can be proved only when hidden records are brought into the open. Freedom of Information Act inquiries have sometimes helped to pierce long-protected secrecy; the process of "discovery" in civil litigation often does likewise.[11]

(3) Re-interpreting the Civil Rights Act

Not all advocates of affirmative action cheat. Some do honestly believe that race preference is permissible under the Civil Rights Act of 1964 when that law is properly interpreted. They argue, in effect, as follows:

> We must be bound by the *spirit* of the law. We must study the history of the Civil Rights Act of 1964 to learn the true intent of Congress in adopting it. Affirmative action programs today advance those Congressional objectives and so, even if they are not strictly "within the letter of the statute" those programs are nevertheless "within its spirit." The aims of Congress [the

argument continues] were to protect blacks, to promote opportunities among minorities for employment and education and public accommodation. Without this Act discrimination against blacks would remain a source of social injustice and unrest. Therefore, when an employer or a union gives employment preference to blacks today, or a university gives admission preference to blacks, that preference cannot be a violation of the Civil Rights Act, because it cannot be the case that Congress intended by that law to prohibit private or public agencies "from taking effective steps to accomplish the goal that Congress designed [the Civil Rights Act] to achieve."[12]

The argument concludes that discrimination that appears to violate Title VII is not discrimination in the eyes of the law if its benefits go to the persons whom that law sought to protect. The argument comes to this:

> The aims of preferential affirmative action are consonant with the aims of Congress. It must be, therefore, that Congress did not intend to forbid such preference. If the literal language of Congress appears to say that it is forbidden, we must interpret that language to mean what it did not say, while saying what it did not mean.

The premise that underlies this argument is false. We are obliged to obey the law as it is written, and judges are obliged to enforce the law as it is written, not as those laws might have been written in view of what we may suppose the purpose of the legislature to have been. The U.S. Congress forbad racial discrimination flatly, and its members understood very well the plain words they used in doing so.[13] Those words, applied with their ordinary and straightforward meaning, make race preference unlawful. A brief review of the legislative history of the Civil Rights Act of 1964, and its language, will make this evident.

One of the objectives of Congress in adopting the Civil Rights Act was to improve opportunities for blacks. It does not follow that Congress did thereby approve every affirmative action plan also having that objective. Parties who share some large objective may differ sharply regarding the steps held permissible to advance it. "The end doesn't justify the means," it is often said, meaning that even very worthy objectives do not justify *any* means believed effective in achieving them. The aphorism is faulty if universalized; some ends do serve importantly in justifying means -- but the moral point of its use here is right: some practices believed useful in broadening employment opportunities for blacks were certainly not approved by the U.S. Congress in the Civil Rights Act of 1964.

Consider this analogy. Suppose Congress, aiming to reduce the use of fossil fuels, appropriated funds to explore alternative sources of energy, but had specifically excluded nuclear energy. What would we say then about the use of the funds to improve nuclear power plants on the ground that (as Justice Brennan had defended minority employment preferences in *Weber*) that use "mirrors" the objectives of the legislature? What the Congress had hoped to achieve is helpful to know; what the Congress explicitly forbad remains controlling.

To insure racial justice for all Congress enacted the Civil Rights Act of 1964. Because opportunities for blacks had long been greatly hindered by racial discrimination, a central theme of that legislation was the explicit prohibition of discrimination in employment. It is wrong-headed to argue that Congress cannot have intended to forbid discrimination against whites, because some discrimination against whites might also advance opportunities for blacks. When the Civil Rights Act is interpreted in such a way as to suggest that under it preferences for some minorities are lawful, that Act is being used to justify precisely what it was designed to condemn.

When the Civil Rights Act of 1964 was held to permit preference by sex to counteract sex imbalance in the work force of a county agency in California, Justice Scalia cited again that passage from Title VII noted above,[14] To use the Civil Rights Act to defend the very discrimination it condemns, he continued, converts Title VII "from a guarantee that race or sex will not be the basis for employment determinations, to a guarantee that it often will." Such reasoning, he observed, "effectively replace[s] the goal of a discrimination-free society with the quite incompatible goal of proportionate representation by race and by sex in the workplace."[15]

(4) The Intentions of Congress in the Civil Rights Act of 1964

The intent of a legislature becomes a matter of importance when the application of some statute requires its interpretation because the wording is ambiguous or its meaning unclear. Unforeseen circumstances may give rise to controversies that the language of the statute does not resolve. To determine how that unclear language should bear upon the newly arisen conditions it is sometimes necessary, therefore, to construe legislative intent at the time of enactment. Or legislation may have been formulated in deliberately ambiguous language in order to win passage, later obliging some court to construe legislative intent to adjudicate the law's application.

No such problems are presented by the Civil Rights Act of 1964. The language of every Title within it exhibits, as the Chief Justice of the Supreme Court later noted, "no lack of clarity, no ambiguity."[16] When any employer deliberately discriminates against an applicant for employment, or against an employee seeking promotion, simply because he is white -- a form of preference now widespread under "affirmative action" -- that, in the unambiguous language of the statute, is "an unlawful employment practice."

Has the Act been interpreted at some point in its history to prohibit discrimination only against blacks but not against whites? No, never.

When whites and blacks have been treated differently the Supreme Court concluded, after close examination of the Act and its legislative history, that it "prohibits discrimination against the white petitioners in this case upon the same standard as would be applicable were they Negroes."[17] Without doubt the Civil Rights Act applies equally to persons of all races.

This consistent application of a single standard to all races has been repeatedly affirmed by the Supreme Court. Unanimously the Court held, in 1971, that "The objective of Congress in the enactment of Title VII is plain from the language of the statute. It was to achieve equality of employment opportunity. . . . Discriminatory preference for any group, minority or majority, is precisely and only what Congress has proscribed."[18] And again, five years later, "Title VII prohibits all racial discrimination in employment, without exception for any group of particular employees."[19] When, three years after that, the issues of racial *ratios* in employment was before the Supreme Court, they concluded:

> It is clear beyond cavil that the obligation imposed by Title VII is to provide an equal opportunity for each applicant regardless of race, without regard to whether members of the applicant's race are already proportionately represented in the work force[20]

With respect to the question of whether the Civil Rights Act protects whites equally with non-whites there is no trace of ambiguity in the law itself or in Supreme Court opinions that have interpreted it. And therefore there is no need to enter the question of legislative intent in enacting this legislation.

Nevertheless the advocates of race preference open that question to advance their reinterpretation of the Act, seeking support for preferences in the legislative history. That history must therefore be re-examined to settle definitively the matter of legislative intent. The question is this: Did Congress intend, when it adopted the Civil Rights Act of 1964, to permit some racial preferences for minorities? The answer is no, absolutely not; the proof of this is overwhelming.

(5) The Evidence Regarding Congressional Intent

The Civil Rights Act of 1964 was debated at great length in both the U.S. House of Representatives and in the U.S. Senate; the full record of those debates is available to us in the *Congressional Record*.[21] Committee reports to the House are open to us.[22] A scholarly study of the legislative history of Title VII has been published.[23] What was intended by the members of Congress in enacting this legislation is fully and definitively determinable.[24]

No reasonable person who has examined these materials can doubt what the intent of Congress was in choosing the words they did choose. Democrats and Republicans both, conservatives and liberals both, insisted repeatedly and at length, illustrating their convictions with detailed examples, that the Civil Rights Act of 1964 (Called H.R. 7152 in the Congressional debates) would forbid *all* racial preference in public settings for *any* race.

The one great objection raised to the Act (and especially to Title VII) in both the House and the Senate was this: using it, opponents alleged, racial proportionality might someday be required by some Federal agency under color of law. An employer (suggested one critical minority report) "may be forced to hire according to race, to 'racially balance' those who work for him in every job classification or be in violation of Federal law."[25] This objection had to be overcome if the bill were to be passed. The fear that racial balance might be imposed under the bill had to be allayed. To this end proponents of the Act forcefully and repeatedly re-assured their colleagues that no such racial balancing was contemplated, that preferential hiring by race could not be required and *would not be permitted* under Title VII. The key section of Title VII was 703(a), which expressly forbad all racial discrimination, and all racial classification that would have any adverse impact upon any single employee. It reads:

It shall be an unlawful employment practice for an employer —

(1) to fail or refuse to hire or to discharge any individual, or otherwise to discriminate against any individual with respect to his compensation, terms, conditions, or privileges of employment, because of such individual's race, color, religion, sex, or national origin; or

(2) to limit, segregate, or classify his employees or applicants for employment in any way which would deprive or tend to deprive any individual of employment opportunities or otherwise adversely affect his status as an employee, because of such individual's race, color, religion, sex, or national origin.

When the debate in the House of Representatives opened early in 1964 the Chairman of the House Committee on the Judiciary, Rep. Emmanuel Celler (D-NY), clarified the intent of this critical passage. The fear that it would require or permit hiring or promotion on the basis of race, he said, resulted from a description of the bill that was "entirely wrong." Even a court, he continued:

could not order that any preference be given to any particular race, religion, or other group, but would be limited to ordering an end to discrimination. The statement that a Federal inspector could order the employment and promotion only of members of a specific racial or religious group is therefore patently erroneous. . . . The Bill would do no more than prevent a union, as it would prevent employers, from discriminating against or in favor of workers because of their race or religion or national origin. It is likewise not true that the Equal Employment Opportunity Commission [EEOC] would have the power to rectify existing "racial or religious imbalance" in employment by requiring the hiring of certain people... simply because they are of a given race or religion. Only actual discrimination could be stopped.[26]

This emphatic declaration of intent echoed repeatedly during the debate in the House. Rep. Lindsay (D-NY, later to become Mayor of New York City) took up the defense of the Act:

> This legislation does not . . . as has been suggested heretofore both on and off the floor, force acceptance of people in schools, jobs, housing, or public accommodations because they are Negro. It does not impose quotas or any special privileges of seniority or acceptance. There is nothing whatever in the bill about racial balance. . . . What the bill does do is prohibit discrimination because of race.[27]

With that very clear understanding the bill passed the House, 290-130, on February 10, 1964.

In the Senate the expression of legislative intent was equally unequivocal but much more voluminous. Again the chief objection of opponents was that some federal inspector might one day require racial balancing under color of law. Again -- and again and again and again and again -- the defenders of the bill replied with unqualified reassurance, vehemently insisting that such fears were totally unfounded. The key word, appearing repeatedly in the bill, was "discrimination." That word was examined minutely on the Senate floor. Could it be taken to mean the absence of racial balance? Answer by the proponents: definitely not. Could it be intended as a technical term, whose hidden meaning was "discrimination against blacks but not discrimination against whites"? Answer: certainly not. The majority leader and foremost advocate of the bill in the Senate, Hubert Humphrey (Democratic candidate for President in 1968), put that suggestion permanently to rest:

The meaning of racial or religious discrimination is perfectly clear. . . . it means a distinction in treatment given to different individuals because of their different race, religion, or national origin.[28]

The only freedom of employers that the bill limits, he emphasized, is the freedom to take action based on race, religion, sex, or national origin. Repeatedly the supporters of the civil rights bill were obliged to reply on the Senate floor to the objection that the bill would lead or might lead to race preference. Not so, they said, not *possible*. Senator Humphrey again:

That bugaboo has been brought up a dozen times; but it is nonexistent. In fact, the very opposite is true. Title VII prohibits discrimination. In effect it says that race, religion, and national origin are not to be used as the basis for hiring and firing. Title VII is designed to encourage hiring on the basis of ability and qualifications, not race or religion.

He goes on to give examples that make clear what is implicit throughout the whole of Title VII; namely, that employers may hire and fire, promote and refuse to promote for any reason, good or bad, provided only that individuals may not be discriminated against because of race, religion, sex, or national origin.

He repeats himself in the hope that none will fail to hear:

The truth is that this Title forbids discriminating against anyone on account of race. This is the simple and complete truth about Title VII.[29]

Senator Kuchel (R-Calif), the Minority Whip and a strong supporter of the Civil Rights Act, explained why the seniority of workers already employed would not be affected by the Act:

Employers and labor organizations could not discriminate in favor of or against a person because of his race, his religion, or his national origin. In such matters the Constitution, and the bill now before us drawn to conform to the Constitution, is color-blind.[30]

Senators Clark (D-PA) and Case (R-NJ) were floor captains in the Senate for Title VII. Specifying what that Title did or did not prohibit or permit was one of their tasks. It was their duty to refute the charge that Title VII might result in preference for any group. They prepared a memorandum for the Senate, expressing the intent of Title VII unequivocally:

> Any deliberate attempt to maintain a racial balance, whatever such a balance may be, would involve a violation of Title VII because maintaining such a balance would require an employer to hire or to refuse to hire on the basis of race. It must be emphasized that discrimination is prohibited as to any individual.[31]

The Department of Justice prepared a separate memorandum on the same aspect of the Act, presenting the same conclusion about the force of its language:

> No employer is required to maintain any ratio of Negroes to whites, Jews to Gentiles, Italians to English, or women to men. The same is true of labor organizations. On the contrary, any deliberate attempt to maintain a given balance would almost certainly run afoul of Title VII because it would involve a failure or refusal to hire some individual because of his race, color, religion, sex, or national origin. What Title VII seeks to accomplish, what the civil rights bill seeks to accomplish, is equal treatment for all.[32]

The opponents of the bill did not trust these assurances. Senators Smathers (D-FL) and Sparkman (D-AL) granted that the bill did not require the use of racial quotas, but complained of its likely indirect effects. Under this bill, they suggested, employers might be coerced by federal agencies into giving preference by race. Could the proponents guarantee that this would not be permitted? The response, given by Senator Williams (D-RI) is painful to read today. Opponents of the Civil Rights Act, he said,

> "persist in opposing a provision which is not only not contained in the bill, but is *specifically excluded* from it. Those opposed to H.R. 7152 [the Civil Rights Act] should realize that to hire a Negro solely because he is a Negro is racial discrimination, just as much as a "whites only" employment policy. *Both forms of discrimination are prohibited by Title VII of this bill.* The language of that Title simply states that race is not a qualification for employment. . . . [A]ll men are to have an equal opportunity to be considered for a particular job. Some people charge that H.R. 7152 favors the Negro at the expense of the white majority. But how can the language of equality favor one race or one religion over another? Equality can have only one meaning, and that meaning is self-evident to reasonable men. Those who say that equality means favoritism do violence to common sense."[33]

But the fear that the proposed legislation might somehow permit or encourage race preference would not down. Again the floor leader, Senator Humphrey, was obliged to reiterate the intent and the plain meaning of the words of the Act:

> The Title [Title VII] does not provide that any preferential treatment in employment shall be given to Negroes or to any other person or groups. It does not provide that any quota systems may be established to maintain racial balance in employment. In fact, the title would prohibit preferential treatment for any particular group, and any person, whether or not a member of

any minority group, would be permitted to file a complaint of discriminatory employment practices.[34]

In the face of this parade of unequivocal accounts of the intent of the act by its authors, marching across the printed record of its adoption, it cannot now be plausibly maintained that race preference for minorities is 'within the intent' of this Civil Rights Act. But the defenders of preference have nevertheless sought to do so, next relying upon the following maneuver: Congress may have intended to forbid preference to *maintain* balance (the argument goes) but they did not intend to forbid preference designed to *eliminate existing imbalance*. Preferential affirmative action now is of the latter sort, and that sort of preference really is within the intent of the law.[35]

The distinction is spurious. Senators Clark and Case had written in their joint memorandum:

> Title VII would have no effect on established seniority rights. Its effect is prospective and not retrospective. Thus, for example, if a business had been discriminating in the past and as a result has an all-white working force, when the title comes into effect the employer's obligation would be simply to fill future vacancies on a non-discriminatory basis. He would not be obliged — or indeed permitted — to fire whites in order to hire Negroes, or, once Negroes were hired, to give them special seniority rights at the expense of white workers hired earlier.[36]

The Justice Department, in its analysis of the Act, also emphasized that Title VII could not be used to alter seniority entitlements because of earlier discrimination in employment:

> [E]ven in the case where, owing to discrimination prior to the effective date of the Title, white workers had more seniority than Negroes ... assuming that seniority rights were built up

over a period of time during which Negroes were not hired, these rights would not be set aside by the taking effect of Title VII. Employers and labor organizations would simply be under a duty not to discriminate against Negroes because of their race.[37]

A distinction between "achieving racial balance" and "maintaining racial balance" was never any part of the understanding of Congress in adopting the Civil Rights Act. The claim that preference is now lawful in the light of that distinction is therefore groundless. For Congress in 1964, as the Civil Rights Act was debated, race preference was simply impermissible, and would be wrong if undertaken with the one aim or with the other. Moreover, it is evident that current defenders of preference are as ready to use such devices to maintain racial balance as to achieve it — so that argument resting upon that distinction is completely without merit. Race preference for any purpose flies in the face of this law.

To meet the repeated objections of implacable opponents, the sponsors of the Civil Rights Act decided to insert an amendment that would lock the matter down, making it impossible for some federal agency later to use the law as justification for some race preference. Senators Dirkson (R-IL) and Mansfield (D-MT) devised a sub-section, 703j, specifically addressing the fear of imposed racial balancing. This Section provides that *nothing in the law may be interpreted to require* giving preference to any individual because of his race.[38]

In an ironic turn, this section was later used by defenders of preference in the following way. Noting that the added section bars the *requirement* of racial preference, but does not specifically prohibit racial preference, it was argued that it must have been the intention of Congress to permit race preference if it were not required. The inference is utterly disingenuous. The added section was designed specifically to meet the objection that race preference might someday be required. It did not address "voluntary" race preference for the very good reason that voluntary race preference of every kind had been repeatedly and specifically forbidden by the plain language of the sections above it. No one in Congress imagined that race preference could be lawful under this statute if adopted by an employer "voluntarily," when it clearly says:"It shall be an unlawful employment practice for an employer to discriminate against any individual . . . to limit, segregate, or classify . . . in any way that would deprive any individual of opportunities. . . because of race, color, sex, or national origin."[39] "Voluntary" preference — preference given by the employer, or the employer and the union, without court compulsion, was precisely what proponents and opponents in Congress understood to be flatly forbidden by the unambiguous wording of Section 703(a), which banned any employment practice that would discriminate against any individual because of that person's race. The prohibition was not repeated in Section 703(j) because it would have been redundant to do so, and because it would have diluted the force of that specially added section aimed narrowly at the objection that race preference might some day be imposed by government.

The difference in the phrasing of Sections 703(a) and 703(j) makes clear the difference in their targets and functions. The general prohibition of preference, Section 703(a), is addressed to employers and begins: "It shall be an unlawful employment practice for an employer. . ." But section 703(j) is addressed to possible enforcement agencies and courts and therefore begins with words plainly meant for them: "Nothing in this subchapter shall be interpreted to require. . ." To infer that Congress did not intend to prohibit preference from the fact that this added Section does not repeat the prohibition already explicit in the preceding sections is transparently unsound.

After Section 703(j) had been inserted the debate on the Senate floor continued. Defending Title VII (with 703(j) included) Senator Saltonstall (D-MA) summed up its full meaning:

"the legislation before us today provides no preferential treatment for any group of citizens. In fact, it specifically prohibits such treatment."[40]

Still the skeptics remained unsatisfied. Senator Ervin (D-NC) suspected that the act "would make the members of a particular race special favorites of the laws." Senator Cooper (R-KY) replied, again seeking to put Ervin's suspicions to rest:

"As I understand Title VII, and employer could apply the usual standards which any employer uses in employing, in dismissing, in promoting, or in assigning those who work for him. There would be only one limitation: he could not discriminate, he could not deny a person a job, or dismiss a person from a job, or promote on the sole ground of his color, or his religion, other factors being equal."[41]

Senator Clark, answering Senator Ervin more emphatically, said, "The bill does not make anyone higher than anyone else. It established no quotas." The normal judgment of employers, he continued, would continue to rule in their own business activity — but:

"all this is subject to one qualification, and that qualification is to state: 'In your activity as an employer, as a labor union, as an employment agency, you must not discriminate because of the color of a man's skin.' that is all this provision does ... It merely says, 'When you deal in interstate commerce you must not discriminate on the basis of race.'"

Then, to avoid any possible misinterpretation, Senator Clark repeated himself:

"All it [Title VII] does is to say that no American, individual, labor union, or corporation, has the right to deny any other American the very basic civil right of equal job opportunity."[42]

Today, more than half a century after the adoption of the Civil Rights Act, anyone who argues that some race preference is "within the intent" of that Act must be ignorant of its legislative history. There is no evidence that would support a construction of that Act under which preference might be lawful. Scour those thousands of pages of *The Congressional Record* as I have done, and one finds not a single speech, not one account of the proceedings of that historic summer, that can support the claim that race preference under the law might afterward be lawful. If there were any such passage that might contribute even in some strained way to the defense of preference we can be sure it would have been fastened upon by its contemporary advocates and much repeated. But they never mention such a passage because it does not exist.

One explicit exception to its prohibitions Congress did make, and very narrowly marked off. Section 703(i) permits certain preferences to Indians living on Indian reservations:

> Nothing contained in [Title VII] shall apply to any business or enterprise on or near an Indian reservation with respect to any publicly announced employment practice of such business or enterprise under which preferential treatment is given to any individual because he is an Indian living on or near a reservation.[43]

The great care with which this exception is set forth confirms the judgment that if there had been any other exceptions they would have been made no less precisely, and that, absent such explicit qualifications, the prohibition of race preference in the Civil Rights Act was intended to apply to all. No other exceptions appear in the Act.

The form of this argument logicians call "modus tollens"; by lawyers it is sometimes called a "negative pregnant." Re-stated simply it goes like this: If Congress had intended to permit private or "voluntary" race preference by universities or labor unions or corporations they would surely have expressed that intention explicitly in the law. No such expression, either in the act itself or in the debates preceding its adoption, is to be found. Therefore Congress cannot plausibly be supposed to have had that intent.

Justice Thurgood Marshall, writing for the Supreme Court in a later analysis of the intent of Congress in adopting the Civil Rights Act, quotes Rep. Celler in the 1964 debates, who said then that the Act was intended to "cover white men and white women and all Americans."[44] Citing Senators Humphrey, Clark, Case, and Williams in passages like those quoted here above, Marshall (a defender of affirmative action) concludes: "Its [Title VII's] terms are not limited to discrimination against members of any particular race." This conclusion he further substantiates by extended reference to the interpretation of Title VII given by the Equal Opportunity Employment Commission. The EEOC, writes Marshall,

> whose interpretations are entitled to great deference, . . . has consistently interpreted Title VII to *proscribe racial discrimination against whites on the same terms as racial discrimination against non-whites,* holding that to proceed otherwise would constitute a derogation of the commission's Congressional mandate to eliminate all practices which operate to disadvantage the employment opportunities of any group protected by Title VII, including Caucasians.[45]

This history of legislative intent in adopting the Civil Rights Act, said Thurgood Marshall then, is "uncontradicted."

Is the horse dead, or may we flog it yet again? Racial discrimination thrives today in every college and university giving preference in admission, in every private corporation giving preference in hiring and promotion, in every government agency giving favor in licensing and in contracting, and so on. The law of the land is being widely ignored, shamefully violated. So it is not unreasonable to report here once again what the understanding of the United States Congress was in the final hours of its long debate in that summer of 1964. The Senate would decide the matter. The decision was at hand. Advocates took their final opportunity to present their understanding of the bill they knew was about to pass: Here are two of those final statements, characteristic of most of the rest:

> Senator Muskie (D-ME): It has been said that the bill discrimi-nates in favor of the Negro at the expense of the rest of us. It seeks to do nothing more that to lift the Negro from the status of inequality to one of equality of treatment.[46]

> Senator Moss (D-UT): The bill does not accord to any citizen advantage or preference; it does not fix quotas of employment or school population; it does not force personal association. What it does is to prohibit public officials and those who invite the public generally to patronize their businesses or to apply for employment, to utilize the offensive, humiliating, and cruel practice of discrimination on the basis of race. In short, the bill does not accord special consideration; it establishes equality.[47]

Very self-consciously, aware that it was making history, the Senate passed the amended civil rights bill on June 19, 1964, by 73 to 27, every member voting. The bill was then returned to the House, approved as amended, and signed into law by President Johnson as the Civil Rights Act of 1964. It was the product of one of the most protracted and most intense legislative struggles in the history of the United States. The meaning and force of every line and every phrase in the Act had been scrutinized, argued, and explained with scrupulous care. The legis-lators knew precisely what they were prohibiting, and we know exactly what they understood themselves to be prohibiting because they took care, very deliberately, to put their explanatory accounts on record.

The subsequent history of what has been called "affirmative action" must give some pain to every honest American.. Racially preferential schemes in our universities and in private industry have been widely adopted, sometimes in response to threats by the Office of Federal Contract Compliance. Even in contexts in which non-discrimination had been honestly and scrupulously respected the allegation of "under-utilization" has forced -- still does force in some places -- hiring by ethnic numbers, and all the preferences that racial balancing entails.

One of the most tenacious opponents of the Civil Rights Act, Senator Sparkman of Alabama, a racist, repeatedly warned that no matter what was promised by its defenders, federal agencies would misuse the Act to give preference to minorities. He was hooted down on the floor of the Senate. He countered to his colleagues: You may be confident that the "suggestion" will be made to some small business that may have a small government contract that if it does not carry out the prefer-ences proposed to the company by some inspector, its government contract will not be renewed.[48] To our shame we have proved that racist prescient.

No honest and impartial person — administrator, employer, or judge — may now in good conscience defend the claim that the Civil Rights Act of 1964 was intended by Congress to permit preference by race. Preference by race is wrong; plainly and indubitably it is a violation of federal law.

End Notes -- Chapter 5

1   The whole of the Civil Rights Act of 1964 may be found in chapter 42 of *United States Codes*. The passages cited here are identified by Section number, within their respective Titles.

2   Section 703(j) of Title VII.

3   Justice Antonin Scalia in *Johnson v. Transportation Agency*, 480 U.S. 616, 1987.

4   438 U.S. 265, 1978. A much more detailed examination of this case appears in the next chapter, in which constitutional arguments regarding race preference are considered.

5   Sec. 601, Title VI, cited by Justice Stevens in *Bakke* at p. 412.

6   *Bakke* at p. 418.

7   18 California 3d, p. 55.

8   This statute has given rise to a chain of much-discussed Supreme Court cases involving a small company called Adarand Constructors, whose low bid on a small highway project in Colorado was rejected in favor of a higher bid by a minority-owned sub-contractor, because the general contractor would receive a cash bonus as a consequence of that minority ownership. The matter first reached the highest court as Adarand Constructors v. Pena, in which the very strict standard governing the use of racial categories that has long been applied to the several states was applied to the Federal government as well. The devices used by the U.S. Department of Transportation in dealing with contractors have been repeatedly altered to protect the preferences deviously, making the preferences themselves and the agency that advances them slippery targets.

9   *Bakke* at p. 418.

10   The instruction was included in the letter sent to the applicant by the Equal Employment Specialist, as reported in *Heterodoxy*, March, 1993. "Equal" in this context, generally means something like "Unequal."

11   A Freedom of Information Action request to the University of Michigan, of which I was the author in 1995, resulted in the disclosure of documents proving that the University's earlier denials of race preferences in admissions had been deceptive or dishonest. Data revealed in those documents, reprinted in *The New York Times*, led to two Supreme Court cases, *Gratz v. Bollinger* (539 US 244) respecting preferences for admission to the undergraduate college, and *Grutter v. Bollinger* (539 US 306) respecting admission practices to the law school. The plaintiffs contended that the race based practices of the University of Michigan were violations of Title VI and of the Constitution. These cases, discussed in detail in Chapter 6, were decided in 2006. Race preferences in admission at other universities have been revealed in a series of reports published by Center for Equal Opportunity, in Washington D.C.

12   This is the argument given by Justice Brennan in holding that the racial preference for blacks given by a labor union and an industrial employer was within the spirit of

Title VII of the Civil Rights Act. The phrases here in quotation marks are the words of Justice Brennan in that case, *Steelworkers v. Weber*, 443 U.S. 193 (1979).

[13] Senator Hubert Humphrey, floor manager for the Civil Rights Act in the Senate, was asked early in the debate what was meant by the word 'discrimination" as it was used in the bill. He answered on the Senate floor as follows:

> "[T]he word 'discrimination' has been used in many a court case. What it really means in the bill is a distinction in treatment.... given to different individuals because of their different race, religion, or national origin.... The answer to this question is that if race is not a factor we do not have to worry about discrimination because of race.... The Internal Revenue Code does not provide that colored people do not have to pay taxes, or that they can pay their taxes six months later than everybody else.... If we started to treat Americans as Americans, not as fat ones, short ones, tall ones, brown ones green ones, yellow ones, or white ones, but as Americans ... we would not need to worry about discrimination." 110 *Congressional Record* 5864, 5866.

Affirmative Action Not What It Seems," *The Michigan Review*, 1 April 1992.

[14] Section 703j of Title VII, noted above at Endnote 2.

[15] Justice Scalia, in *Johnson v. Transportation Agency*, 480 US 616.

[16] Chief Justice Warren Burger, in 1979, dissenting in *Weber*, 443 U.S. 193.

[17] *McDonald v. Santa Fe Trail Transportation Company* (427 U.S. 273) at p. 283.

[18] *Griggs v. Duke Power Company*, 401 U.S. 424 (1971) at p. 431.

[19] *Johnson v. Transportation Agency*, 480 U.S. 616.

[20] *Furnco Construction Corp. v. Waters*, 438 U.S. 567 (1978).

[21] The Congressional debates appear in volume 110 of the *Congressional Record* of 1964, extending intermittently over exactly 13,000 pages of ten massive tomes.

[22] See: *House of Representative Reports*, no. 914, 87th Congress, First Session, 1963. Additional views of particular members, and groups of members, appear there in addition to these reports.

[23] See Francis J. Vaas, "Title VII: Legislative History" in *Boston College Industrial and Commercial Law Review*, vol. 7, pp. 431-458. Vaas wrote: "Seldom has similar legislation been debated with greater consciousness of the need for 'legislative history' or with greater care in the making thereof, to guide the courts in interpreting and applying the law" (p. 444).

[24] In the Senate it was decided to take up the civil rights bill directly, as a body, and so it was not submitted to committee there. The full text of that lengthy Senate floor debate is open to us.

[25] *House Committee Reports*. 1963, p. 69.

26   *The Congressional Record, vol. 110, p. 1,518.*

27   *Ibid,* p. 1540.

28   *Ibid,* p. 5,423.

29   *Ibid* p. 6,549.

30   *Ibid.* p. 6,564.

31   *Ibid,* p.7,213.

32   *Ibid.,* p. 7,207.

33   *Ibid.,* p. 8,921. Emphasis added.

34   *Ibid.,* p. 11,848.

35   The preferential affirmative action plan adopted by Kaiser Aluminum and the Steelworkers Union in the 1970s was defended by Justice Brennan in just this way. That plan, said he, "is not intended to maintain racial balance, but simply to eliminate a manifest racial imbalance." *Steelworkers v. Weber,* 443 U.S. 193, at p. 208.

36   *Ibid.,* p. 7,213.

37   *Ibid.,* p. 7,207.

38   It reads in full: "Nothing contained in this subchapter shall be interpreted to require any employer, employment agency, labor organization, or joint labor-management committee subject to this subchapter to grant preferential treatment to any individual or to any group because of the race, color, religion, sex, or national origin of such individual or group on account of an imbalance which may exist with respect to the total number of percentage of persons of any race, color, religion, sex, or national origin employed by any employer, referred or classified by any employment agency, or labor organization, or admitted to, or employed in, any apprenticeship or other training program, on comparison with the total number of persons of such race, color, religion, sex, or national origin in any community, State, section, or other area,, or in the available work force in any community, State, section, or other area." 42 U.S. Codes 2000e-2(j).

39   The full text of the key section, 703(a), which formulates the prohibition in detail, appears at the outset of this chapter.

40   *The Congressional Record,* 1963, vol. 110, p. 12,269.

41   *Ibid.,* p. 13,078.

42   *Ibid.,* pp. 13,079-80.

43   42 U.S. Codes, 2000(e).

44   *The Congressional Record,* 1963, vol. 110, p. 2,578.

45   *McDonald v. Santa Fe Trail Transportation Co.,* 427 U.S. 273, at pp. 278-280, and 283. Emphasis added.

[46]   *The Congressional Record,* 1964, vol. 110, p. 14,328.

[47]   *Ibid.,* p. 14,424.

[48]   *Ibid.,* p. 8,618.

CHAPTER 6

Race Preference Violates the Constitution

---

(1) The Equal Protection of the Laws

Human slavery was abolished in the United States in 1865.[1] Until that time full democracy was not possible in the United States. The underlying principle of human equality was explicitly incorporated into the Constitution of the United States three years later. All persons, whatever their race or color, are to be recognized as equals. However much we may differ in wealth or strength or wisdom, *before the law* no racial distinctions are recognized here. This guarantee of equality is expressed in the first Section of the Fourteenth Amendment of the U. S. Constitution in a single clause whose forcefulness is matched by its clarity:

> "...nor shall any State...deny to any person within its jurisdiction the equal protection of the laws."[2]

The meaning of these words, and the intent with which they were made part of our Constitution, is no mystery: white supremacy no longer. Any State, or any agency of any State, that gives preference to any group of persons because of their race or color or national origin violates our Constitution. Many laws, including the great Civil Rights Act of 1964 discussed at length in the preceding chapter, implement this prohibition. Race preference cannot stand under our Constitution.

Equality is the philosophical anchor of American democracy. Equality of right — the equal opportunity to participate in the life of the community and to benefit from its laws — is grounded in the fundamental equality of persons. If all are not equal, if some class of persons are thought inferior by nature, the classes will differ in their entitlements. In historical kingdoms they always did. Between nobles and commoners, patricians and plebeians, freemen and slaves, distinctions of class were critical. Where there is no commitment to the fundamental equality of persons democracy cannot be justified, and is unlikely to succeed.

(2) Suspect Classifications and Race Consciousness

Humankind was generally conceived to be, over the course of history, rightly divided into classes, some by nature underlings, others by nature their masters. The systematic oppression of some classes by others was commonly supposed and intellectually respectable. Slavery in America was justified by the assumed inferiority of blacks, persons essentially different from the whites who captured, bought and sold them.

That classification of persons we know to be deeply wrong. How honorable and thoughtful citizens could have defended it we now find it difficult to understand. We are shamed by the days in which, even in our own land, generations of otherwise decent people sorted human beings by arbitrary physical criteria.

Aware of the evil purposes long served by racial classifications we are rightly suspicious of them in every context. In any public place or under any public law -- in commerce or in school or in some government office -- every classification by race is inescapably *suspect*.[3] That is the adjective -- "suspect" -- with which classifications by race are regularly described by the United States Supreme Court.

The equal protection of the laws does not forbid every racial classification. Blacks and others who have been clearly injured by unlawful discriminatory practices may come to our courts for remedy,. and a just remedy may require that the race of persons who were earlier injured be taken into account. To give victims what they are due we may be obliged to use the racial categories by which they had been earlier deprived of what they were due. In one of the justly famous school desegregation cases of the 1970s our Supreme Court agreed that:

> just as the race of students must be considered in determining whether a constitutional violation has occurred, so also must race be considered in formulating a remedy.[4]

The objective remains strictly non-discriminatory, "to eliminate from the public schools all vestiges of state imposed segregation."[5] Consciousness of race may be unavoidable at times but its application to public business remains always problematic. Even when the aim is desegregation, as in those famous school cases of the 1970s, race-consciousness may enter, under our Constitution, only as an unavoidable instrument of justice; no *preference* by race is to be given.

The distinction -- between race consciousness which may be essential in some circumstances to give remedy, and race preference introduced to achieve some inappropriate racial objective -- lies at the center of the constitutional controversy over "affirmative action." The passage from justifiable consciousness of race to unjustifiable preference by race goes often unrecognized; that passage helps to explain the equivocal uses of the phrase "affirmative action."

(3) The Standard of Strict Scrutiny

Every racial classification is rightly suspect. So every use of such a classification must be closely examined to determine whether the constitutional guarantee of equal protection has been violated or preserved. The standard applied is that of *strict scrutiny*. The U.S. Supreme Court has repeatedly insisted that where race is used in a legislative or administrative classification the standard of constitutional permissibility must be the very strictest possible. Very shortly after the enactment of the Civil Rights Act of 1964, Justice Byron White wrote, in a Florida case:

> We deal here with a classification based upon the race of the participants, which must be viewed in light of the historical fact that the central purpose of the Fourteenth Amendment was to eliminate racial discrimination emanating from official sources in the States. This strong policy renders racial classification 'Constitutionally suspect' and subject to *the most rigid scrutiny* ....[I]nvidious official discrimination based on race... bears a heavy burden of justification, as we have said, and will be upheld only if it is necessary, and not merely rationally related, to the accomplishment of a permissible state policy.[6]

Three years later, in 1967, Chief Justice Earl Warren made that point again:

> At the very least, the Equal Protection Clause demands that racial classifications ... be subjected to the most rigid scrutiny, and, if they are ever to be upheld, they must be shown to be necessary to the accomplishment of some permissible state objective, independent of the racial discrimination which it was the object of the Fourteenth Amendment to eliminate.[7]

Warren cited Justice Hugo Black, who had opened his opinion in a famous 1944 case with these words:

It should be noted, to begin with, that all legal restrictions which curtail the civil rights of a single racial group are immediately suspect... courts must subject them to the most rigid scrutiny.[8]

Justice Black had cited a famous passage, authored by Chief Justice Stone and joined by every member of the Court in 1943, that has reappeared in very many decisions since:

Distinctions between citizens solely because of their ancestry are by their nature odious to a free people whose institutions are founded upon the doctrine of equality.[9]

That unanimous Court, in its turn, had cited a decision handed down in 1886, only 21 years after the adoption of the Fourteenth Amendment:

The Fourteenth Amendment to the Constitution is not confined to the protection of citizens. . . . [Its] provisions are universal in their application, to all persons within the territorial jurisdiction, without regard to any differences of race, of color, or of nationality; and the equal protection of the laws is a pledge of the protection of equal laws. It is accordingly enacted by section 1977 of the Revised Statutes that 'all persons within the jurisdiction of the United States shall have the same right, in every state and territory ...to the full and equal benefit of all laws and proceedings ...and shall be subject to like punishment, pains, penalties, taxes, licenses, and exactions of every kind, and to no other.' [10]

In 1978, when the race preferences of the University of California were at issue in *Regents v. Bakke,* Justice Powell, writing for the Court, left no doubt that there would be no departure from that settled principle of constitutional law:

"Racial and ethnic distinctions of any sort are inherently suspect and thus call for the most exacting judicial examination."[11]

In 1995 our highest court reaffirmed the principle that strict scrutiny must be applied to every racial classification, and expanded the reach of that standard; it applies not only to legislation of the several States, but to legislation of the United States Government as well:

> Federal racial classifications, like those of a State, must serve a compelling governmental interest, and must be narrowly tailored to further that interest . . . . When [political judgments regarding the necessity of any classification] touch upon an individual's race or ethnic background, he is entitled to a judicial determination that the burden he is asked to bear on that basis is precisely tailored to serve a compelling governmental interest, the constitution guarantees that right to every person regardless of his background. . . . [A]ny person, of whatever race, has the right to demand that any governmental actor subject to the constitution justify any racial classification subjecting that person to unequal treatment under the strictest judicial scrutiny.[12]

This demand — the application of this settled constitutional principle -- was yet again reiterated in 2001.[13]

Precisely what does the application of strict scrutiny entail? The answer was given in plain words by Justice Powell in 1986:

> There are two prongs to this examination. First, any racial classification must be justified by a compelling governmental interest. Second, the means chosen by the state to effectuate its purpose must be narrowly tailored to the achievement of that goal.[14]

To meet the standard of strict scrutiny, any legislation using a racial classification must serve an interest that is not merely reasonable, or substantial, or even important; its objective must be overriding, *compelling*. And that compelling need must be served clearly and directly, imposing no burdens because of race that do not bear narrowly on that overriding objective.

This demand for a "narrowly tailored" relationship between the law and its purpose is the jurisprudential way of expressing an intuitively clear moral principle: a remedy, to be just, must *fit* the wrong it addresses. If we aim to give redress, what we do must compensate in appropriate form and degree for the injury actually suffered; persons who suffered that injury must be compensated, not some other set of persons who share their skin color or national origin. Any instrument using suspect classifications must be "narrowly tailored" to accomplish the compelling need to which it is said to respond.[15]

This standard of strict scrutiny is meant to be a test that suspect classifications will not easily pass. The Constitutional command that no State may deny to any person within its jurisdiction the equal protection of the laws is to be strictly enforced; no subordinate government or its agency, no state university or other public institution, may be allowed to apply laws differently to persons because they are of different racial groups unless an overriding demand of justice itself requires that differentiation.

There is one purpose generally agreed upon as being a so compelling as to justify the use of racial classifications. Persons to whom a known injury has been done ought be "made whole" for the sake of justice, so far as that is possible. When the injury done had used a racial classification, there may be no way to devise appropriate relief without attending once again to race. In such circumstances a racial classification may prove defensible, but it will be understood as a *remedy*, devised in the light of the injury to be redressed, not as a *preference*. A racial classification when introduced as a remedy will be limited by the context, not universal; it will be addressed to an identified set of deserving persons, not an entire racial group.[16]

Preference awarded to members of some ethnic group simply because they are members of that group can never pass this test of strict scrutiny. Preference cannot satisfy the first prong of the strict scrutiny standard because no state interest is so compelling that it can justify the adverse impact of such preference upon other persons only because of their skin color or national origin. Nor can preference satisfy the second prong of the strict scrutiny standard because no classification drawn simply by skin color or nationality could ever be tailored narrowly to serve a need that is genuinely compelling.

(4) Allegedly Compelling Needs

The justifications most commonly put forward to show the constitutional acceptability of race preference are these:

-- to compensate for societal discrimination and oppression

-- to achieve racial balance in some body

-- to achieve diversity in schools, colleges and other contexts

-- to provide role models for minority students

-- to provide better professional services for minorities

-- to desegregate some public body

-- to integrate some public body

No one of these alleged justifications can pass the test of strict scrutiny set forth in the preceding section. I take them in order:

(4a) Race Preference to Compensate for Societal Discrimination

We saw, in Chapter 4, why race preference cannot be *morally* justified by the demand for compensation. Race cannot justly meet a compensatory need because it will always prove to be both *over*-inclusive, awarding benefits to many who are not entitled to them, and *under*-inclusive, failing to award benefits to many who (even if entitled to relief) are of such a color (or nationality, etc.) that they get nothing. The underlying difficulty is this: color of skin is not itself an injury, and therefore cannot be in itself the ground for preferential remedy.[17]

Those moral considerations, discussed at length in Chapter 4, apply directly in the realm of constitutional principle. Compensation cannot justify race preference (in constitutional terms) because the interest served by race preference is *not compelling,* and because that race preference *cannot be narrowly tailored* to any need shown. The first Section of the Fourteenth Amendment guarantees the equal protection of the laws to every single person *individually.* That guarantee makes a Constitutional defense of race preference impossible. Race preferences are awarded to some group, advantage is given to all persons in that group because of their ethnicity. But the Equal Protection clause protects the rights of persons viewed as individuals, not the rights of any group. They are rights understood distributively, not collectively. Any single individual who is denied some benefit simply because of race will have had his or her rights under the Equal Protection clause infringed.

The oppression of minorities in America is an ineradicable stain on our history. However, that oppression can serve as the constitutionally compelling interest that might justify the use of racial classification only if preference is awarded, as remedy, to persons having suffered identifiable injuries done by identifiable institutions. This is the force of the *individualized* locus of the right to equal protection.

Supreme Court decisions have repeatedly cited the following famous passage, from a 1948 decision, *Shelly v. Kraemer:* "The rights created by the first section of the Fourteenth amendment are, by its terms, guaranteed to the individual. The rights established are personal rights."[18] Race preferences are by their nature awarded to racial groups. But group rights are a fiction. The same right may belong to each member of a group, of course, but the group – "Jews" or "Hispanics" -- cannot be the holder of rights because, under our Constitution, rights are held by individuals. To justify a racial classification in some compensatory way, therefore, it would have to be shown that every member of the preferred racial group did in fact suffer the injury for which redress is proposed. Justice Potter Stewart put it eloquently:

> A judicial decree that imposes burdens on the basis of race can be upheld only where its sole purpose is to eradicate the actual effects of illegal race discrimination. . . .

A judicial decree that imposes burdens on the basis of race can be upheld only where its sole purpose is to eradicate the actual effects of illegal race discrimination. . . . The hostility of the Constitution to racial classification by government has been manifested in many cases decided by this Court. *And our cases have made it clear that the Constitution is wholly neutral in forbidding such racial discrimination,* whatever the race may be of those who are its victims. Under our Constitution, the government may never act to the detriment of a person solely because of that person's race. The color of a person's skin and the country of his origin are immutable facts that bear no relation to ability, disadvantage, moral culpability, or any other characteristics of constitutionally permissible interest to government. 'Distinctions between citizens solely because of their ancestry are by their very nature odious to a free people whose institutions are founded upon the doctrine of equality.' The command of the equal protection guarantee is simple but unequivocal: 'No state shall. . . deny to any person. . . the equal protection of the laws.' [19]

Preference given to some persons over others on the basis of race or national origin, without regard to any injury suffered by the individuals preferred, violates the constitutional rights of those who bear the burden of the preference given.

Defenders of preference contend that advantages given to minorities today are designed to make up for the inequalities of yesterday. So grave and long continued has discrimination against minorities in our country been (they reason), that we can do them justice now only by discriminating *for* them. The moral blunder reappears; the injuries are supposed to lie in skin-color, so that redress is awarded to those having that skin-color. When the Constitution is understood to protect rights held by *individuals,* and to recognize no rights of skin-color groups, the error is exposed.

Defended as compensation, preferences face yet another constitutional barrier: institutions (such as universities) giving such preference do not have the *authority* to use race in this way. The University of California argued explicitly (in *Bakke)* that its admission preferences were justified "to counter the effects of societal discrimination." This argument was rejected by the Supreme Court for the moral reasons given above, but also because no arm of government may use suspect classifications to help once-victimized groups at the expense of others *unless* there have been "judicial, legislative, or administrative findings of constitutional violations"[20] for which redress may be in order. After such findings have been made, the rights of those victimized persons may be entitled to an appropriate remedy devised by a court or a legislature. Without such findings of constitutional or statutory violations no court or government agency can be authorized to take from some for the sake of others. Preferential remedies will necessarily inflict some harm on those not preferred. Without the finding of some earlier violation no government agency can be justified in inflicting such harm. The University of California, as Justice Powell pointed out, "does not purport to have made, and is in no position to make, such findings. Its broad mission is education, not the formulation of any legislative policy or the adjudication of particular claims of illegality . . . [I]solated segments of our vast governmental structures are not competent to make those decisions. . . Before relying upon these sorts of findings in establishing a racial classification, a governmental body must have the authority and capability to establish, in the record, that the classification is responsive to identified discrimination."[21]

Universities do not have the authority to establish such a record; they are not competent to respond appropriately to some earlier violation of law.

This argument devastates even the most well-meaning efforts by universities and like bodies to give redress for what they perceive to have been "societal discrimination" -- a notion described by Justice Powell as "an amorphous concept of injury that may be ageless in its reach into the past."[22] The Constitutional conclusion is framed by the context of the Bakke case, but is widely applicable:

Hence, the purpose of helping certain groups whom the faculty of the Davis Medical School perceived as victims of 'societal discrimination' does not justify a classification that imposes disadvantages upon persons like respondent [Alan Bakke], who bear no responsibility for whatever harm the beneficiaries of the special admissions program are thought to have suffered. To hold otherwise would be to convert a remedy heretofore reserved for violations of legal rights into a privilege that all institutions throughout the nation could grant at their pleasure to whatever groups are perceived as victims of societal discrimination. That is a step we have never approved.[23]

Such a step will never be approved. The authority to make such determinations given to middle-level bureaucrats working behind closed doors would be uncontrollable; it would invite the of preferences use to advance the social vision of those who happen to be in authority. A university, a government agency, a private employer, does not have the authority to give preferences to racial groups because, in its wisdom, such preferences are an appropriate remedy for wrongs long suffered. The compensatory defense of general race preferences, under our Constitution, must fail.

4(b) Race Preference to Achieve Racial Balance

It is often assumed that in the absence of racial discrimination the ethnic profiles -- of student bodies in colleges, and of the work force in business workplaces -- industry would be racially balanced, the percentage of minorities in any given school, or workplace, being roughly equal to the percentage of that minority in the population at large. This assumption is false. Racial discrimination often reinforces race clustering, but patterns of interest and performance are not purely the product of discrimination. Some racial and ethnic grouping is perennial and natural; eliminating every racial imbalance cannot be what justice demands. Efforts to preclude such clustering — are there proportionally too many Jews at the University of Chicago? too many black players in the National Basketball Association? — may be themselves unjust.

The quest for racial balance has nevertheless been put forward as a justification of race preference. The University of California (like many universities) long sought, in its words, to "reduce the historic deficit of traditionally disfavored minorities"[24] in its student body. This objective, plainly honorable, cannot serve, under the standard of strict scrutiny, as the compelling objective that might justify race preference. The racial imbalance complained of may result from decisions freely made by members of the minorities themselves. To assume that minority members would act as those in the racial majority do, in proportions much like theirs, is as patronizing as it is unwarranted.

Using that assumption as the implicit ground for an allegedly compelling need is unsound. Justice Powell, addressing this argument in *Bakke,* disposed of it crisply:

> If petitioner's [the University of California's] purpose is to assure within its student body some specified percentage of a particular group merely because of its race or ethnic origin, such a preferential purpose must be rejected not as insubstantial but as *facially invalid.* Preferring members of any one group for no reason other than race or ethnic origin is discrimination for its own sake. This the Constitution forbids.[25]

But the claim that preference is justified by the need for racial balance continues to reappear. In Jackson, Michigan, the School Board, joined by the teachers union, defended race preference for minority public school teachers on the alleged ground that minority teachers were "substantially and chronically underrepresented." That argument, relying upon arithmetic ratios to justify preference, was rejected by the U. S. Supreme Court.[26]

The goal in that case was a ratio of black teachers to white teachers that would mirror the ratio of black students to white students. But the factors governing the availability of teachers are much different from those affecting the racial profile of student populations; the racial proportionality sought was unattainable. The School Board nevertheless protected minority teachers [defined as "employees who are black, American Indian, Oriental, or of Spanish descendancy" (sic) against layoff even when white teachers with higher seniority had to be laid off in their stead. Explicit preference by race was given by the Board to "minority-group personnel."

The contract provided that until proportionality sought was reached the proportion of black teachers was not to be allowed to decline;

layoffs (not uncommon in a school district) had always to be of white teachers. The effect was that of a contractual ratchet, the unattainable target pushing the proportion of minority faculty ever upward. The seventh layoff of a high-seniority white teacher in this district led to Supreme Court review. Blacks at that time constituted 9.7% of the Michigan population. The percentage of minority faculty in the Jackson schools was 13.5%, the proportion of minority administrators was 19.6%, the proportion of minority coaches was 18.3%, and the proportion of minority teaching aides was 29.6%. But the proportion of black students in that district was still higher, and teaching ratios were to mirror student ratios, so even the most junior minority teachers were never threatened by a budget-imposed system-wide layoff. Only white teachers could lose their jobs, and they did.

Justice Sandra Day O'Connor noted in the oral argument of this case that the Court would seek to determine "whether the government can demonstrate a compelling state interest to justify such a [racial] classification." She then asked: "Now what is the compelling state interest that the School Board asserts here? Is it to maintain faculty-student ratio, or is it some other purpose? What do you rely on today?" The Board's attorney replied that the need for "integration" and the need for a "diversified faculty" were both motivating factors. The oral exchange then continued:

Justice O'Connor: So the Board does rely essentially on a faculty-student ratio and the role-model rationale?

Attorney for the Board: Justice O'Connor, I didn't say that and I didn't mean that. I think what I was looking at specifically was, was it their duty to integrate, how to go about that integration.

Justice O'Connor: Integrate in hiring. You are talking about hiring employees?

Attorney for the Board: . . .If you're not going to do something about layoffs is it going to be considered by the public as a good faith effort to integrate?

Justice O'Connor: Maybe I can't get an answer, but I really would like to know what the compelling state interest is that you are relying on for this particular layoff provision, in a nutshell.

Attorney for the Board: [Swimming!] . . .to protect the gains made that was going to allow us to do that as we looked at what we certainly thought were some of the factors we ought to be looking at like faculty and wanting a diverse ethnic faculty, to protect that we had to have [the layoff provision].

Justice O'Connor: To protect a faculty-student ratio that the Board thought was appropriate?

Attorney for the Board: . . .We wanted them there. We had to have a method of protecting them.[27]

That desire cannot serve as a compelling interest that would justify race preference in circumstances like these. The Jackson schools were well integrated; minority teachers were employed there in substantial numbers. The School Board and the Union had simply sought a numerical proportion that they considered an ideal racial balance.

Imbalance in the New York City public schools has created a new drive for preference. There are eight specialized high schools in NY to which admission is greatly prized but won only through performance on a competitive examination, the Specialized High School Admissions Test (SHSAT). Of the available slots in these schools in the year 2018, Asian students had won 52.5%, white students 28%, Latino students 6.5% and black students 3.8%, according to the City's Department of Education, as reported in *The Wall Street Journal*, 13 June, 2018. The imbalances are painful but undeniably the result of different performance on admission exams. To overcome those imbalances by giving outright preference in the grading of racial groups is plainly unacceptable. Alternatively, the elimination of all admission exams has been considered; this would hide the imbalance, but would profoundly change those schools. Is that the right path for the New York City schools? The Mayor has proposed an alternative response that is plainly devised to give preference to the black and Latino students who seek admission but whose performance on the SHSAT has been inferior. He would have the city *set aside* 20% of the admissions to these schools for minority students who have not done well enough on the admissions test. Those students would then be obliged to complete a summer session called the "Discovery Program" earlier devised for "disadvantaged" students. Race preference takes many forms.

When a racial distribution that matches some pre-selected goal is taken to be the only proper standard, and marked departure from that ratio is taken to be evidence of discrimination, the use of numbers becomes insidious.[28] Proportionality is not to be expected everywhere; patterns of work and interests and skills, patterns of residence and styles of life, differ greatly among ethnic groups for reasons having nothing to do with discrimination. Ethnic proportionality is an unsuitable standard for social justice, and is certainly not a constitutional justification of race preference.

(4c) Race Preference to Achieve Diversity

Diversity — of opinion, of perspective, of background and interest — is in general a good thing. Arguments that conflict, reports and attitudes that vary, enrich the democratic process. Ethnic diversity too, when it brings different perspectives on controversial issues, is a worthy

objective in some contexts. But ethnic diversity does not insure intellectual diversity; persons of different races often hold similar views,
and there is likely to be as much diversity of view within a given ethnic
group as among groups. In some spheres -- in the study of logic for example, or chemistry -- diversity is not important. In other contexts, in
a religious seminary for example, diversity may have no place. Mindful
of such limitations, most colleges and universities do understandably
seek a diverse student body.

The race preferences adopted by colleges (and employers and government agencies) were not originally introduced because of their
contribution to diversity. Race preferences have been mainly defended
as instruments "to level the playing field," or as devices to advance
racial balance. These justifications, as the courts made clear, cannot
provide a constitutional defense. So advocates of race preference
turned to diversity as their allegedly compelling need.

Ordinary people are not likely to think that diversity, even where a
genuine value, is an interest rightly described as "compelling." Some
healthy communities are ethnically homogenous. Open inquiry does
not require researchers of varied nationalities or races. University administrators sometimes contend that the diversity critical for higher
education can be achieved only through ethnic variety. The University
of Michigan, for example, while defending its race preferences before
the Supreme Court, published in 1999 a collection of essays entitled
"The Compelling Need for Diversity in Higher Education."

There is an historical explanation for this extravagant claim. As the
justification of race preference as minority compensation was being
rejected by the Supreme Court in Regents v. Bakke, Justice Powell, having agreed that the preferences in question were a violation of the
equal protection clause, sought to soften the absolute preclusion of
racial considerations that had been demanded by the earlier opinion
of the California Supreme Court. To this end he pointed out that some

constitutional interests are furthered by the intellectual diversity of college classes which, he emphasized, is much more than racial diversity. In considering the merits of individual applicants, he suggested, it would not be unreasonable for an admissions officer to consider race as a "plus factor" in the effort to achieve diversity. Race might be weighed, he thought, but only in evaluating the contributions of particular applicants. That sort of racial consideration for the sake of diversity would differ sharply, he believed, from the race preferences awarded by the University of California then (and many universities today) which exhibit on their face the intention to discriminate generally by race.

This introduction of "diversity" into the discussion of university admissions appeared in Justice Powell's opinion only; it was not joined or even mentioned in the opinions of the other eight justices in that landmark case. Needing some constitutional defense for their practice, universities came to rely on Powell's discussion of diversity. It became the "compelling need" that the justification of race preference requires.

This matter remains controversial. Justice Powell's views were incorporated in the majority opinion of the Court in *Grutter v. Bollinger* in 2003 (539 U.S. 306). Four of the Justices of the Supreme Court (Justices O'Connor, Kennedy, Scalia, and Chief Justice Rehnquist) expressed in 2002 their outright rejection of the diversity justification in the realm of broadcast journalism, emphasizing that racial classifications may be used by government, if at all, only to respond to a demand of justice. They wrote:

> Modern equal protection has recognized only one [compelling state] interest: remedying the effects of [identified] racial discrimination. The interest in increasing the diversity of broadcast viewpoints is clearly not a compelling interest. It is simply too amorphous, too insubstantial, and too unrelated to any legitimate basis for employing racial classifications.[29]

Justice Clarence Thomas joined the Court after that 1990 case had been decided, but he has repeatedly expressed his strong objections to race preference, and there is little doubt that he would have joined those four in rejecting the diversity defense.[30]

The diversity argument relies upon a factual claim -- the alleged benefit of ethnic diversity in classrooms — that is disputable. Empirical evidence submitted by the University of Michigan purportedly showing the great benefits of preference has been subjected to careful review by social scientists and statisticians. The claim of the university, that great educative improvement is produced by student ethnic diversity, has been found probably false. One set of critics concluded, after meticulous review of what is known in this sphere, that the University's empirical claims about the educational benefits of racial diversity is simply unwarranted, its own data not supporting the conclusion that campus racial diversity is correlated with positive educational outcomes.[31] The study upon which the University relied as evidence was submitted to a second detailed examination,[32] and was found not to meet minimal standards of research design and methods -- measurement, sampling, and statistical interpretation.[33] The University's factual claim that student diversity yields overriding educational benefit is not warranted.

In this controversy the critical empirical test employed is a well-established statistical technique called multivariate analysis, commonly applied to complex settings with many variables to determine where causality may be reliably inferred. Examining the data used by the University of Michigan, the National Association of Scholars concluded that multivariate analysis "actually disconfirmed the claim that campus racial diversity is correlated with educational excellence."[34]

But empirical doubts about the benefits of diversity are secondary to a more fundamental point: however great such benefits may be they cannot justify discrimination.[35] Diversity is not a compelling state interest.

Even if it were thought to be a critical need, preference by ethnic group cannot be tailored to meet that need. Under the standard of strict scrutiny, diversity as the constitutional justification for race preference must fail.

(4d) Race Preference to Provide Role Models for Minorities

The role model justification of preference has been categorically rejected by the Supreme Court. That justification was advanced by a school board in 1986 to defend preferences in the employment of minority teachers. The Court held that such a defense is really no more than one variant of the defense based on "societal discrimination" discussed earlier. Minorities (on the role model theory) have been relegated to employments in lower economic strata. To support and encourage their employment in more prestigious positions it is essential that minority children have, as role models, teachers who are themselves minority members. Without such role models, it is argued, there is too little self-esteem among minorities to support the needed changes.

The Court pointed out that this is simply another way of contending that societal discrimination of an earlier day justifies race preference today. The majority opinion rejecting the argument was authored by Justice Powell:

> This Court has never held that societal discrimination alone is sufficient to justify a racial classification. Rather, the Court has insisted upon some showing of prior discrimination by the governmental unit involved before allowing limited use of racial classifications in order to remedy such discrimination.[36]

Any "role model theory" ignores the need for that direct relationship. Powell writes:

[T]he role model theory employed by the District Court has no logical stopping point. The role model theory allows the Board to engage in discriminatory hiring and layoff practices long past the point required by any legitimate remedial purpose.

As a claimed justification of preference it therefore fails to satisfy the requirement that it be a compelling need. It also fails to satisfy the requirement that any racial classification be narrowly designed to address the purported need. Powell continues:

Moreover, because the role model theory does not necessarily bear a relationship to the harm caused by prior discriminatory hiring practices, it actually could be used to escape the obligation to remedy such practices by justifying the small percentage of black teachers by reference to the small percentage of black students. Carried to its logical extreme, the idea that black students are better off with black teachers could lead to the very system the Court rejected in Brown v. Board of Education.[37]

Powell sums up:

Societal discrimination, without more, is too amorphous a basis for imposing a racially classified remedy. The role model theory announced by the District Court and the resultant holding [reversed in this decision] typify this indefiniteness . . . No one doubts that there has been serious racial discrimination in this country. But as the basis for imposing discriminatory legal remedies that work against innocent people, societal discrimination is insufficient and over expansive. In the absence of particularized findings, a court could uphold remedies that are ageless in their reach into the past, and timeless in their ability to affect the future.[38]

Providing minority role models cannot serve, under the standard of strict scrutiny, to justify race preference.

(4e) Race Preference to Yield Better Professional Services for Minorities.

Race preference in professional school admissions had been confronted by the Supreme Court several years before the *Bakke* case reached them. At the University of Washington a preferential admissions policy had been devised in the law school, it was argued, in order to provide better legal services for minorities in the state of Washington.[39] White lawyers generally tend to serve white clients; if black clients are to be adequately served, (the law school contended) black lawyers must be produced to serve them. A similar argument was presented in *Bakke* to support minority admission preferences to the Davis Medical School. Preference was claimed essential to produce the black doctors who are most likely to provide the health care needed in black communities.

The argument was rejected by the Supreme Court. Good professional service does not entail that it be rendered by persons of any given skin color. Black doctors and black lawyers may be more likely than white doctors and white lawyers to build their practices in black communities, but it does not follow that preferring blacks in admission to law and medical schools is the right way to address the need for better professional service.

In *Bakke* Justice Powell addressed this argument explicitly. Even were the State's interest in facilitating health care so compelling as to support the use of a suspect classification, he wrote, there is no evidence that a university preferential admissions program is needed to promote the goal of better service, or is in any way designed to achieve it. Powell quotes the Supreme Court of California which had written:

The University concedes it cannot assure that minority doctors who entered under the program, all of whom expressed an
interest in practicing in a disadvantaged community, will actually
do so. It may be correct to assume that some of them will carry
out this intention. . . Nevertheless, there are more precise and
reliable ways to identify applicants who are genuinely interested
in the medical problems of minorities than by race. An applicant
of whatever race who has demonstrated his concern for disadvantaged minorities in the past and who declares that practice
in such a community is his primary professional goal would be
more likely to contribute to alleviation of the medical shortage
than one who is chosen entirely on the basis of race and disadvantage. In short, there is no empirical data to demonstrate that
any one race is more selflessly socially oriented or by contrast
that another is more selfishly acquisitive.[40]

Preference by race cannot be shown to improve health care, or legal
services. There has been no showing that racial classifications are likely
to have any significant effect on the quantity or quality of service received by minority communities. Black clients can be well served by
lawyers of every color; Hispanics, when sick, do not require Hispanic
physicians; white defendants can be fairly tried before black judges.
The supposition that conscientious fulfillment of professional function
is dependent upon sameness of race or heritage between client and
practitioner is false and destructive. The record of professional services completely transcending difference of race or religion or nationality
is long and honorable.

Moreover, defending race preference on the basis of the professional
needs of minorities assumes, tacitly, that minority lawyers and doctors
will devote themselves to ethnically exclusive practices. This may be
true for many, but the expectation that professional practices will be
generally limited in this way is worse than parochial — it exerts heavy
and unfair pressure on minority professionals.

Finally, some will contend that there is a need felt by minority group members for lawyers (and doctors) of their own race and cultural heritage, who are sensitive to their attitudes and circumstances, who share their spirit and who alone can make them comfortable. This is a very troubling defense of preference. If "comfort" really were a satisfactory ground for race preference, firms with a clientele largely of one color might rely on their supposed comfort to discriminate openly against job applicants of some other color. "Our black clients cannot be comfortable with white attorneys [we may hear] and good professional service to our clients requires their psychological confidence. That is possible only with community of heritage." This was the argument long used to justify discrimination against minority professionals. It will be welcomed by bigots of every color.

The belief that the professional needs of persons of a given race are fully met only by persons of the same race mistakenly suppose a unity and distinctness of interest shared by all members of that racial category. The variety among blacks, and among whites, is thus submerged by racial identification. We are urged, with good intentions, to think with our blood.

The response to this argument was given by one of the most liberal justices of the Supreme Court, William O. Douglas, a graduate of the Washington Law School who was angered by that school's defense of its racially discriminatory admissions program. When the Court held, in *DeFunis v. Odegaard* (416 U.S. 312, 1974) that the complaint of Marco DeFunis was moot since he was soon to graduate from the Washington Law School, Douglas dissented vigorously, writing:

> The state, however, may not proceed by racial classification to force strict population equivalences for every group in every occupation, overriding individual preferences. The equal protection clause commands the elimination of racial barriers, not their creation in order to satisfy our theory as to how

society ought to be organized. The purpose of the University of Washington cannot be to produce Black lawyers for Blacks, Polish lawyers for Poles, Jewish lawyers for Jews, Irish lawyers for the Irish. It should be to produce good lawyers for Americans.[41]

(4f) Race Preference to Desegregate some Public Body

In the public schools racial segregation plainly violates the U.S. Constitution.[42] For a unanimous Supreme Court Chief Justice Earl Warren wrote, in Brown v. Board of Education, 1954 (called Brown I):

> Education. . . is a right which must be made available to all on equal terms. . . Does segregation of children in public schools solely on the basis of race, even though the physical facilities and other 'tangible' factors may be equal, deprive the children of the minority group of equal educational opportunities? ... It does.
> [I]n the field of public education the doctrine of 'separate but equal' has no place. Separate educational facilities are inherently unequal. Therefore... the plaintiffs and others similarly situated . . . are, by reason of the segregation complained of, deprived of the equal; protection of the laws guaranteed by the Fourteenth Amendment.[43]

In the public schools desegregation, the *elimination* of any system of governmentally authorized separation by race, was held a requirement of justice. Separate facilities are inherently unequal facilities, and therefore to segregate by race is to deprive some of their rights under the Equal Protection Clause. Desegregation in such contexts plainly is a compelling state interest.

But race *preference* was never envisaged as an instrument to combat segregation, and cannot serve that end. On the contrary, preference (for whites!) was precisely what had to be rooted out. Only months after *Brown* was decided a set of related cases arose, called Brown II,[44] in which the Court addressed the need to implement desegregation. How was the right to non-discriminatory admission to the public schools to be secured? Courts were directed to use their powers in equity to review the plans proposed by previously segregated school systems, and thus to effect the "elimination of a variety of obstacles in making the transition to school systems operated in accordance with the Constitutional principles set forth in Brown I" The lower Federal courts were ordered "to take such proceedings, and to enter such orders and decrees. . . as are necessary and proper to admit to public schools on a racially nondiscriminatory basis."[45] No preference by race was dreamed of in these implementing cases, none was suggested, and none was permitted.

The struggle to make desegregation a reality was long and bitter. The unambiguous command to desegregate the public schools was defied, or evaded, by school systems all over the American South. In Charlotte, North Carolina, for example, fifteen years after *Brown I* had outlawed state imposed racial segregation, two-thirds of the black students attended 21 schools whose students were 100% (or 99%) black. Double sets of racially identifiable schools were duplicitously maintained in single systems, deliberately administered so as to maintain the wrongful segregation of pupils on the basis of race. That had to be stopped.

"[T]o break up the dual school system" that had been deliberately maintained, and "to eliminate from the public schools all vestiges of state-imposed segregation," the district courts found some race-conscious remedies an unavoidable necessity. Drastic remedies, subsequently approved by the Supreme Court in *Swann v. Charlotte-Mecklenburg School District* (402 U.S. 1) were needed to right those long continued wrongs: non-contiguous school zones were paired and grouped. Busing -- the much hated transport of elementary school pupils, blacks to formerly white schools and whites to formerly black

schools -- was ordered and approved "as one tool of school desegregation."[46] That was affirmative action in the original sense of that term
— positive steps to achieve desegregation without a hint of preference by race. The implementing measures were indeed race conscious
because only in that way could remedy be provided for earlier wrongs
done by the state. The Supreme Court wrote:

> Absent a constitutional violation there would be no ground
> for judicially ordering assignment of students on a racial ba-
> sis. All things being equal, with no history of discrimination,
> it might well be desirable to assign pupils to schools near-
> est their homes. But all things are not equal in a system that
> has been deliberately constructed and maintained to enforce
> racial segregation. The remedy for such segregation may be
> administratively awkward, inconvenient, even bizarre in some
> situations, and may impose burdens on some; but all awk-
> wardness and inconvenience cannot be avoided in the interim
> period when remedial adjustments are being made to elimi-
> nate the dual school systems.[47]

The constitutional legitimacy of such race-conscious remedies at that
time gives no warrant for the claim that the desegregation of the public schools now justifies any preference by race. Equal treatment for all
was precisely and only what was ordered.

All of the so-called "school cases" of the 1960s and 1970s were decided in that spirit of remedy for earlier identified wrongs by the States. In
1978, when the University of California argued that those earlier cases
could serve as precedents for its system of admissions preference,
Justice Powell, looking back, rejected the argument flatly. He wrote:

> Each [of the earlier school desegregation cases] involved
> remedies for clearly determined constitutional violations. E.g.
> *Swann v Charlotte-Mecklenburg Board of Education* 402 U. S. 1

(1971); *McDaniel v. Barresi,* 402 U.S. 39 (1971); *Green v. County School Board,* 391 U.S. 430 (1968). Racial classifications thus were designed as remedies for the vindication of constitutional entitlement.[48]

But when that remedy has been administered, and the discriminatory segregation by school boards has at last been overcome, the use of race in the assignment of students could no longer be justified. The procedures of the Charlotte-Mecklenburg School District were overseen by the courts for more than thirty years. In 2001 the Court of Appeals for the Fourth Circuit upheld a lower court ruling that that school district was now "unitary," no longer unjustly segregated, and that, therefore, the refusal by administrators of that district to assign a student because of her race to a school to which she was otherwise qualified, could not be justified under the Constitution.[49]

The circumstances of plaintiffs like Alan Bakke who are burdened by state uses of race are, as Justice Powell observed in a footnote, "wholly dissimilar" to that of a pupil bused from his neighborhood school in compliance with a desegregation decree. The University of California did not arrange for Mr. Bakke to attend a different medical school in order to desegregate the Davis Medical School. On the contrary, the University "denied him admission and may have deprived him altogether of a medical education."[50]

In sum: desegregation cannot serve as the constitutional justification of race.

(4g) Race Preference to Integrate Some Public Body

Integration and desegregation are very different. The nondiscriminatory admission of all students to public schools, their desegregation, is a right constitutionally guaranteed. Desegregating public schools is a constitutional command. Integrated schools, schools in which pupils of different races enroll in fact, are widely and rightly sought as ideal. An integrated school system must be desegregated, of course — but a desegregated school district may not be integrated, or fully integrated, for reasons having nothing to do with state action or state policy.

In recent years the ideal of racial or ethnic integration has been rejected by some minority groups who do not wish to become a part of a mixed or blended community that is mainly white. The dream of Martin Luther King, Jr., that black and white might live and work and study together, attending not to skin color but to the content of character, was deeply honorable. I share it. But not all blacks, or all whites, share it now.[51]

Many religious minorities are quite deliberately parochial, fearing that the integration of their students with those of the majority may sap the vitality of their convictions, or may corrupt (from their point of view) the religious upbringing of their children. The goods and evils of parochial schools need not be addressed here. Segregation in the public schools is strictly forbidden, but parents may (and often do) seek out residential communities in which the preponderant ethnic heritage is that of their own religion, their own nationality, or their own race, in order that their children may be deeply imbued with those traditions. This is not always wrong. Even those who think such self-separation unfortunate must agree that it is not a practice that violates the Constitution, and certainly not a practice that must be uprooted in order that constitutional values be safeguarded.

In the decades that have elapsed since school busing and other vigorous remedies were introduced to break down segregated school systems, some communities, having achieved integration, have self-segregated themselves once again. The loss of school integration resulting from unforced residential patterns, however much we may not like it, is not proof of deliberate segregation by any public body. Unless that re-segregation can be shown to be the product of state action it is not an injury that can justify a racially preferential remedy.

One illustration: A Federal district court long ago found that the schools in Oklahoma City were intentionally segregated; a school busing plan was eventually devised, ordered (in 1963), and implemented to demolish the dual system. Schools there were desegregated. Many years later, when that busing plan was finally dropped, attendance in many elementary schools began to return to the racially clustered pattern of their residential neighborhoods. Some parents then sought to have the original remedial decree re-instituted. But the Federal district court concluded, after a careful review of the local situation, that the later residential racial patterns were a result of private choice, and not of deliberate segregation, and that, therefore, the school busing order could no longer be justifiably forced upon that school system. This conclusion was ultimately upheld by the U.S. Supreme Court in 1991:

> From the very first, Federal supervision of local school systems was intended as a temporary measure to remedy past discrimination.... [School desegregation] decrees are not intended to operate in perpetuity...Dissolving a desegregation decree after the local authorities have operated in compliance with it for a reasonable period of time properly recognizes that 'necessary concern for the important values of local control of public school systems dictates that a Federal Court's regulatory control of such systems not extend beyond the time required to remedy the effects of past intentional discrimination.[52]

By 1985, racial clustering in Oklahoma City was so attenuated that it could no longer be rightly called a "vestige" of earlier school segregation. The school board there had long maintained the unitary status of the system in good faith, and had sought to implement a neighborhood assignment plan that "was not designed with discriminatory intent." In such circumstances, now fairly common in our country, the Supreme

Court concluded that ". . .the previous injunctive decree should be vacated and the School District returned to local control."[53] When "the vestiges of *de jure* segregation had been eliminated as far as practicable" (as in Oklahoma City decades after the original desegregation decree) a race conscious order, even one that does not give preference, is no longer justifiable.

Desegregation is a constitutional obligation; integration is not, and cannot be forced upon a community whose members freely choose not to embrace it. We may hope for the eventual racial integration of our communities and their school systems. But the race-conscious remedies of the 1960s and 1970s were required for the desegregation of the public schools, not their integration. Integration cannot justify race conscious devices (like school busing) that are not preferential; it therefore cannot possibly serve as the compelling need that might justify race preference under the standard of strict scrutiny.

In sum: Bearing the standard of strict scrutiny in mind, and reviewing the application of this standard by the U. S. Supreme Court to the various defenses of preference that have been put forward for decades, we may confidently conclude that naked preference violates the Constitution of the United States. We have seen that race preference is morally wrong (Chapter 4), and wrong because it breaks the law (Chapter 5). It is Constitutionally wrong as well.

End Notes -- Chapter 6

[1] The Thirteenth Amendment to the U.S. Constitution, ratified in 1865, reads in full:
Section I. Neither slavery nor industrial servitude , except as a punishment for
crime, whereof the party shall have been duly convicted, shall exist within the
United States, or any place subject to their jurisdiction.
Section 2. Congress shall have the power to enforce this article by appropriate
legislation.

[2] Ratified in 1868, the Fourteenth Amendment has five Sections: the second deals
with the apportionment of representatives; the third, with qualifications for Federal
office; the fourth, with the validity of public debt; the fifth gives Congress the power
to enforce the whole. The first Section of the le amendment, in which is formulated
the principle that renders race preference unconstitutional, reads in full:
All persons born or naturalized in the United States, and subject to the jurisdiction
thereof, are citizens of the United States and the State wherein they reside. No
State shall make or enforce and law which shall abridge the privileges or immunities
of citizens of the United States; nor shall any State deprive any person of life, liberty,
or property, without due process of law, nor deny to any person within its jurisdiction the equal protection of the laws.

[3] Classification by "race" is to be taken here, and in all that follows, as shorthand for
all suspect classifications: by national origin, or sex, or color, or religion, and so on.

[4] *Swann v. Charlotte-Mecklenburg Board of Education,* 402 U. S. I. at p. 45 (1971).

[5] Ibid, at p. 6.

[6] *McLaughlin v. Florida,* 379 U.S. 184, (1964), at pp. 192, 196.

[7] *Loving v. Virginia,* 388 U.S. 1 (1967), at p. 11.

[8] *Korematsu v. U.S.* 323 U.S. 214, at p. 216.

[9] *Hirabayashi v. United States,* 320 U. S. 81, at p. 100. Emphasis added. Years later, in
1963, Justice Tom Clark held what was called "the minority transfer rule" unconstitutional, observing that "racial classifications are obviously irrelevant and invidious."
Goss v. Board of Education of Knoxville, 373 U.S. 683. And Justice Potter Stewart, in
that same year, noted that (in the light of *Brown v. Board*) classification on racial lines
is in itself, "per se," impermissible. "A segregated school system ... is invalid simply
because our Constitution presupposes that men are created equal, and that therefore racial differences cannot provide a valid basis for government action." *Abington
School District v. Schempp,* 374 U.S. 203, at p. 317.

[10] *Yick Wo v. Hopkins,* 118 U.S. 356, at p. 369.

[11] *Bakke.* at p. 291.

[12] *Adarand Constructors v. Pena,* 515 U.S. 200, at p. 235 (1995).

[13] *Adarand Constructors v. Mineta,* 534 U.S. 103 (2001).

[14] *Wygant,* 246 U.S. 267

[15] The moral arguments presented earlier in chapter 4 are in this way incorporated into American Constitutional history.

[16] The most illuminating illustration of this distinction is *Franks v. Bowman Transportation Company*, 424 U. S. 727 (1976). In this case the known black victims of racial discrimination by a trucking company sought, as a remedy, to be placed in the seniority lists of that company where they would have been placed if they had not been earlier victimized. To give them that remedy required, of course, that the existing seniority ranking of white employees be adversely affected. But the court rightly held that to give the remedy to which these plaintiffs were entitled, there was no way to avoid classification by race. Only in that way could those injured be made whole, for otherwise they would remain subordinate to persons who, had it not been for racial discrimination in that company, would now be their juniors. Those who were adversely affected by the remedy (even though possibly innocent themselves) had plainly benefited, in seniority, from the specific discriminatory practice for which remedy was being given. Justice clearly requires that persons be awarded what is rightly theirs, and since in such a case the racial classification is critical, its use, although of course subject to strict scrutiny, remains defensible.

[17] See Chapter 4, above.

[18] 334 U.S. 1, at p. 22.

[19] *Fullilove v. Klutznick*. 448 U. S. 448 (1980).

[20] *Bakke*, p. 307.

[21] Ibid, p. 309.

[22] Ibid, p. 307.

[23] Ibid, p. 310.

[24] Brief of the University of California in *Bakke*, cited by Justice Powell at p. 306.

[25] *Bakke* at p. 307. Emphasis added.

[26] See: *Wygant v. Jackson Board of Education*, 476 U.S. 267 (1986).

[27] Official Transcript of Proceedings before the Supreme Court of the United States, 6 November 1985, p. 30.

[28] To make such invidious uses of race counting impossible in California, the American Civil Rights Coalition there sought to place on the state ballot an initiative that would amend the California constitution so as to *prohibit* state and local government from classifying individuals on the basis of race.

[29] *Metro Broadcasting Inc. v. FCC*, 497 U.S. 612 (1990)

[30] See Chapter 4, Section (4), above.

[31] See: Thomas E. Wood and Malcolm J. Sherman, *Race and higher Education: Why Justice Powell's Diversity Rationale for Racial Preferences in Higher Education Must Be Rejected*, National Association of Scholars, Princeton, NJ, 2001.

32   The University of Michigan solicited essays from its own faculty and others to support its claims, and with these produced a book entitled (of course!) *The Compelling Need for Diversity in Higher Education.* Ann Arbor, 1999.

33   See: Robert Lerner and Althea K. Nagai, *A Critique of the Expert Report of Patricia Gurin in Gratz v. Bollinger,* Center for Equal Opportunity, Washington D.C., 2001.

34   Wood & Sherman, op. cit.

35   In 1954, the States defending segregated schools in *Brown v. Board of Education* submitted a great deal of evidence claiming to show that segregation was good for minorities and for majority alike. The state of Virginia (in a companion case) "presented 4 educators, a psychiatrist, and 2 psychologists," all "eminent men" — including the chairman of the psychology department at Columbia University — whose work was supported by "other outstanding scholars" and who testified that "segregated education at the high school level is best for the individual students of both races." Several years before that, in the case that resulted in the first integration of public universities *(Sweatt v. Painter),* the state of Texas had presented evidence aiming to show that segregated education was much better for those segregated. A sociological expert testified: "a very large group of Northern Negroes came South to attend separate colleges, suggesting that the Negro does not secure as well-rounded a college life at a mixed college, and that the separate college offers him positive advantages; that there is a more normal social life to the Negro in a separate college; that there is greater opportunity for full participation and for the development of leadership; that the Negro is inwardly more 'secure' at a college of his own people." A unanimous Supreme Court, finding racial classification in education unacceptable and unjustifiable, gave that evidence the attention it deserved. They ignored it.

36   *Wygant v. Jackson Board of Education,* 476 U.S. 267 (1986).

37   *Ibid.*

38   *Ibid.* Emphasis in the original.

39   *Defunis v. Odegaard,* 416 U.S. 312 (1974). Marco DeFunis was the white plaintiff in this case. When he prevailed in the lower court, he was admitted to the law school by order of that court. By the time his case reached the U.S. Supreme Court he was about to graduate from the law school; the University allowed in oral argument that his performance there had been good and that they would not eject him even if the preferential admissions system were upheld. The Supreme Court thereupon found that nothing in that case remained at issue, and held the case moot.

40   18 California 3d, p. 56.

41   *DeFunis v. Odegaard,* 416 U.S. 312, at p. 342.

42   *Brown v. Board of Education,* 347 U. S. 483. 1954.

43   *Ibid.*

44   349 U. S. 294 (1954).

45   *Ibid.* Emphasis added.

46 *Ibid.* The courageous district court judge in the *Swann* case was James McMillan, a man of finest character and intellect (now deceased) whom the present author is proud to have known.

47 *Swann*, at p. 45.

48 *Bakke*, p. 300.

49 *Belk v. Charlotte Mecklenburg Board of Education*, 2001.

50 *Bakke*, p. 300, footnote 39.

51 In *Kwanzaa and Me: A Teacher's Story* (Harvard University Press, 1995) an experienced elementary school teacher, Vivian G. Paley, raises seriously the question of whether white schools (or "integrated" schools) are bad for black children. One black professor of sociology (she reports) told her that he would "rather have his child go to an all black school, no matter how bad, than to an integrated school." Another black professor (she reports) refuses to send his daughter to a white school because he won't have her feeling "dumb and ugly." Such views are extreme and may be mistaken — but their growing currency shows that racial integration is certainly not a universal ideal.

52 *Board of Education v. Dowell*, (1991).

53 *Ibid.*

Part Three:
Why Race Preference is Bad

Chapter 7:
Race Preference Is Bad for the Minorities Preferred

Chapter 8:
Race Preference Is Bad for the Universities that Give Preference

Chapter 9:
Race Preference is Bad for the Society as a Whole

CHAPTER 7

Race Preference is Bad for the Minorities Preferred

We turn from wrongness to badness.

Race preference is thrice wrong as we have seen. But many who admit this will say that some unfairness must be tolerated because minority support is so sorely needed. Preference for racial minorities, even when somewhat unfair, produces very good results, they say, and these good results outweigh its negatives.

But race preference is not good. It divides the society in which it is awarded. It corrupts the institutions in which it is practiced. It is very bad for us all. And its worst consequences are the injuries it inflicts upon the racial minorities preferred.

Some individual members of those minorities are benefited by preference. But the minority as a whole is undermined. Preference throws doubt on distinguished minority achievement. It imposes upon every member of the preferred minority the demeaning burden of presumed inferiority. Preference *creates* that burden; it makes a stigma of the race of those who are preferred by race. An ethnic group given special favor by the community is marked as needing special favor to succeed -- and the mark is borne prominently by every one of its members. Racial stereotypes are reinforced; the malicious imputation of inferiority is inescapable because it is tied to the color of skin.

Competitive appointments, promotions, and admissions, in institutions of all kinds, are now substantially influenced by consideration of the race of competing applicants.[1] This is generally acknowledged. Preferences embedded in competitive systems have bad consequences for minority candidates. If they are unsuccessful the outcome is a disgrace. Among successful minority candidates who succeed many -- not all, but we cannot know which -- occupy their places because of their race. This cannot be openly acknowledged because it is humiliating. Vague references are made to "affirmative action hiring," or to "special admissions" programs. Such appointments or admissions are not based exclusively upon race, but the substantial weight given to skin color is often the critical factor that accounts for success. It follows that many appointments (admissions, promotions, etc.) are made with a reduced regard for skills or attainments; many who receive such appointments would not occupy their present places had they been white. It is painful to point this out but it is true, and everyone knows, although not everyone will admit, that it is true. The evidence for its truth has been compiled and lamented by blacks as well as whites.[2]

In law schools and medical schools race preference is nearly universal; admission is commonly awarded to minority applicants less well qualified than their majority counterparts. Some are admitted who, had they been white, would have been summarily rejected, not even seriously considered for admission. The statistical gap between the past performances of those admitted on normal competitive criteria, and those admitted preferentially, is wide. Consider:

In 1992, 7.3 percent of all those admitted to medical schools in this country were black. The Association of American Medical Colleges reported that the mean scores for accepted blacks that year were as much as 18% lower than the mean scores of accepted whites, and as much as 4% lower than the scores of white applicants who were *rejected* for admission.[3] The editor of *The Journal of Blacks in Higher Education*, (JBHE) acknowledging extensive preference for black medical school applicants, puts it this way: "Over half the 15,000 white students rejected for admission to U.S. medical schools scored above the mean for black students who were admitted. . . Affirmative action plays a huge, almost determinative role in the admission of African Americans to professional schools."[4] Can a medical student be proud of having been admitted on that basis?

Selective undergraduate colleges also give substantial admission preference by race. At eight Ivy League schools (Brown, Cornell, Columbia, Dartmouth, Harvard, Princeton, University of Pennsylvania, and Yale) admissions officers were interviewed by the editors of *The Journal for Blacks in Higher Education;* statistical data about applicants and matriculants in these schools were then correlated with Scholastic Aptitude Tests, which remain the best predictors of academic success. Using Harvard as illustrative of the preferences given at the most selective institutions, the editor of *JBHE* wrote:

> "We know for certain that in the freshman class that came to Harvard College in the fall of 1991 the mean SAT score of black entering freshmen was 160 points below the average of admitted whites. [Maximum possible combined score, verbal and quantitative, was then 1600.] Admitted blacks averaged combined scores of 1290, whites averaged combined scores of 1450. . . . Very few black students score at this level. Only 102 blacks [nationwide] had scores above 750 on either the math or verbal SAT in 1992, but over 15,000 whites scored at that level."[5]

Colleges far less selective than Harvard give preference to applicants with dark skins. The California Department of Education reported several years ago that "the mean academic scores of blacks are so low that fewer than 5% of black students have the grades necessary to enter the University of California system."[6] To overcome that obstacle, double standards became the rule in California.

Minority students admitted because given preference are less well prepared to succeed in the studies undertaken. They generally perform at a lower level than their peers admitted without preference, and are sometimes cruelly humiliated. Special tutoring is commonly offered to preferred students; remedial courses are designed for them; affirmative action counselors are hired to guide and support them. The intellectual gap arising over 17 years of life is to be closed, it is hoped, in a summer or a semester, but success is spotty and the attrition rate is high. Special dispensations are given so that those preferentially admitted do not wash out early. In medical schools, to avoid an embarrassing failure rate, minority students are commonly given the opportunity to re-take examinations several times; preferentially admitted minority students must somehow be graduated.

That will not happen if standards remain high and the same standards are applied to all. Therefore, if the affirmative action goal is to be reached, either standards do not remain high or the same standards are not applied to all. The gap between the performance of those admitted on established academic merit and those admitted with heavy reliance on race is wide, so the inadequacies of specially admitted students must be overlooked, leniency shown in their evaluation. By hook or by crook minority lawyers, doctors, or bachelors of arts must be got through. In many professional schools minority students rarely flunk out. Everyone -- instructors, roommates, competitors, the students themselves -- knows what is going on. The colleges and professional schools are corrupted; but worse, minority students are demeaned.[7]

After being admitted by race, minority students who cannot compete successfully must be preferred internally. In law schools, for example, "making law review" is a prize hard won, the achievement of only the most accomplished students. Race preference has changed this. The great law reviews have adjusted their standards in response to the pressure for more 'diversity.' In 1992 the Michigan Law Review adopted a policy designed to insure the same percentage of minorities on its staff as in the Law School."[8] It works like this: Applicants' writing is graded blindly; applicants' grade point average in completed law classes is then factored in. Unmodified by race this competition would yield law review appointments thought racially "unbalanced," so ethnic preferences are introduced to fix the results. The policy reads:

> "If [the standard, race-blind] procedures fail to identify a sufficient number of minority candidates for positions on the Law Review, we will supplement these procedures by considering an applicant's affirmative action eligibility . . . that is, on the basis of whether an applicant is a Black American, Mexican American, Native American, or Puerto Rican raised on the American mainland."

Minority students are identified (by the Law School office) as having "affirmative action eligibility" and this is noted on their writing entries. In the end, "a sufficient number of positions will be offered to those applicants from minority groups with the highest writing scores or augmented grades."[9] What number is "sufficient" is not specified, but the essence of the policy is clear: when minority applicants aren't good enough to make it on their own, the best minority applicants available will be appointed to insure the racial numbers sought. To avoid the risk of dreadful embarrassment by the appointment of persons utterly incompetent, the Michigan Law School affirmative action policy concludes with the following proviso: "Positions will not be offered to applicants who score a zero in the writing competition and whose grades fall below a threshold to be determined by the Editor-in-Chief and Managing Editor."

What would one expect the impact of this policy to be upon the spirit of black law students? I report the responses of one outstanding black law student, a former student of mine, identified here only by his initials, MKF. Having done very fine work his first year, MKF was appointed to the editorial board of the Law Review on merit. There he learned of a preferential system for editorial appointments, newly proposed by his fellow board members. Much distressed, he explained to them its consequences for black students:

> First, the reputation of all black students who make law review, whether by preference or by merit, is undermined within and without the school. In the competition for jobs, he observed, "law review" on a minority student's resume [now] signifies merely that one did not both write a competition piece worthy of a zero and fall below a minimum grade point average of an unknown level."[10]

Within the law school minority law students [appointed as editors] face explicit doubt in the eyes of non-review students, and resentment from white students who applied but were not accepted. In the eyes of other minority students, MKF wrote, "the credibility of minority Review members is impeached." Even in their own eyes minority students who rely upon affirmative action preference must

> "live with their own doubt. Meeting the Law Review challenge is a frightening experience. How much more difficult is it for minority students who have reason to believe that they wouldn't have qualified but for their race? How scary it is for one who can think, as many Review members have thought, 'I'm not good enough for this.'"[11]

Those who fail to make the Review, although their "affirmative action eligibility" had been duly noted, are devastated.

Second, minority students are taught a very destructive lesson. MKF continues:

> "Minority students in general are assumed to be less quali-fied than the white applicants. And to the extent that we are, we are told by the Law Review that we need not work hard to develop ourselves as other Law Review hopefuls do; the Law Review will take us for less. Instead of expecting excel-lence from minority students, and in turn minority students expecting excellence from ourselves, we need only expect to be average. (That's a guess, of course; how low the Review will go is a secret.) In this way the Law Review offers little incentive to work hard to make it."

> "Personally," [MKF concludes] "I'm tired of having my achieve-ments doubted. When my wife told her workmates that I had been accepted by the U of M law school, one person muttered, 'it's no wonder, he's black and he's blind.' [MKF's vision is seriously impaired.] On the Law Review I thought I could attain recognition for my merit rather than my color.... Unfortunately, my member-ship is tainted.... Isn't it ironic to have blind grading tickets for everyone and colored grading tickets for minorities? Sometimes I wonder whether I deserve to be on the Editorial Board or whether I stand as a token for our progressive Law Review."[12]

At another law school one black student wrote:

> "I'll never forget my first week of law school. The message was clear: we were the 'slow" kids. A meeting between the dean and a group from my section confirmed this. That experience left no one with the illusion that we were anything but charity cases. We wanted to compete but apparently the law school had some doubt that we could. We were only there for diver-sity's sake."[13]

In engineering as well as in law the product of preference is bitterness. A minority mechanical engineering student in his fifth year at Michigan writes poignantly: "Nobody expects you to know what you're doing.... You're always the last lab partner picked."[14]

Preference humiliates even at the highest levels. When a black administrator, Dr. Yolanda Moses, was appointed President of the City College of New York in 1993 she was correctly described by *The New York Times* as a "little known vice-president from California."[15] A professor at Penn State University observed that this description made "Dr. Moses appear an affirmative action appointment"[16] -- and everyone knows what that means.

Some of those appointed on racial grounds are just not up to the job, and that proves highly embarrassing, as illustrated by the following true anecdote. Two black women were routinely assigned the task of editing a manuscript submitted to the *Harvard Law Review* in 1993; the President of the *Review* at that time, Ms. Emily Schulman, called the assignment a disaster. Her problem was this: The manuscript in question had been submitted by a black assistant professor at the Harvard Law School (who later became a full professor there) and was to be his tenure article, the piece upon which his career might depend. Was she to allow this fine author's work to be edited by persons whose competence as editors she knew to be doubtful? Ms. Schulman understood how race had infected the appointment of editors at the *Harvard Law Review*, so she took it upon herself to investigate the actual capacity of the women assigned to do the requisite editorial work. That investigation provoked outrage on all sides at the law school, especially among its black students. Preference demoralizes everyone involved, and demeans the group preferred.

When preference is given to some ethnic group every member of that group is marked as one likely to have received preference -- whether or not special favor had in fact been given, and whatever the true level of achievement. A black gastroenterologist from New York, Carlyle Miller, whose native ability won him scholarships to Columbia University and to Cornell Medical School, resentfully called affirmative action "a one-way ticket." As a medical specialist you may prove your abilities beyond doubt and win appointments without favor. No matter, says he, "All along the way everyone is questioning you."[17] In Cleveland, an outstanding high school student, valedictorian of her graduating class, was recruited by the best colleges in the country -- but their message to her was degrading. "I should have been the kind of person that anybody would have wanted in their college [she observed] but the letters almost always read 'Dear Black Student....'"[18] An 18-year veteran of the Chicago police force, repeatedly denied promotion to sergeant while Hispanics and females with lower scores than his were given the higher-ranking positions set aside for those groups, observed that, since he himself is black, when at last he gets his promotion that achievement is likely to be so tainted by affirmative action that he will be perceived as (in his own words) a "quota sergeant."[19] An assistant corporation counsel in Chicago reported that, having worked in an Eastern law firm for 18 months, he was never sure whether he was, in his words, "an affirmative action hire," but he always felt like one.

> "You always want to believe that you were hired because you were the best. You work seven days a week, you wear Brooks Brothers suits, you play golf. But everything around you is telling you were brought in for one reason: because you were a quota.... No matter how hard I worked or how brilliant I was, it wasn't getting me anywhere. It's a hell of a stigma to overcome."[20]

Advocates of preference who believe they are doing minorities a great favor must suppose that those they patronize are simply insensitive. Stephen Carter, a professor at the Yale University Law School, puts it like this: "[A]s long as racial preferences exist, the one thing that cannot be proved is which people of color in my generation would have achieved what they have in their absence."[21] The psychological impact of preference upon those preferred is epitomized in the remark of a black student at the University of California: "I feel like I have AFFIRMATIVE ACTION stamped on my forehead."[22]

Admissions and appointments are competitive because the intellectual demands to be confronted -- in hospitals or law firms or colleges -- are great. Scholars are evaluated incessantly -- by their peers, their students, their clients, their patients, their readers. Intellectual mediocrity cannot be hidden. Ethnic preference may lower the intellectual qualifications for admission or appointment, but it cannot lower the standards by which performance -- in the operating room, in court, on the lecture platform — is ultimately judged.

When affirmative action seeks to award with preference what only intellect can achieve, it forges a link between minority status and weak performance. The claim that minorities are intellectually inferior is a canard, utterly false. But that claim is what preference encourages. Preferential affirmative action, well meant, has done more in recent years to damage the intellectual reputation of minorities than entrenched bigotry.

Do this thought experiment. Suppose that height were made a critical consideration in university admissions. Suppose preference were widely given, in law schools or undergraduate colleges, to overcome the disadvantage that short stature is taken to impose. Absurd, but suppose it. Some short applicants, minimally qualified, would be admitted because of that extra credit given to all shorts. Then shorts overall would, as a group, prove to be weaker students, because many of them, marginally qualified, were not so well suited for academic work as their peers who were selected on grounds related only to attainment or promise. With remedial instruction, patient tutoring, some wincing and some winking, the specially admitted shorts are pushed through to graduation somehow. Charts showing the growing numbers of shorts in the student body and among the faculty are displayed by administrators who express pride and satisfaction in the increased numbers of short professionals admitted and graduating, while insisting that much work remains to be done to further improve the "stature numbers."

Some of the very most talented applicants and graduates will of course always be short; there is no conflict between shortness and intellectual excellence. But where shortness had been systematically introduced into the selection process it must necessarily dilute the importance of intellectual excellence. The shorts will be poorer students as a group, not because they are short, but because they (unlike the non-shorts) are on average selected on a lower intellectual standard; that is what preference by height entails. Everyone soon learns that the credentials of noticeably short students, or short doctors, or short lawyers, are suspect. Suspicion will burden all shorts because no one can be sure — not even the shorts themselves — whether their selection for some demanding position was made wholly in virtue of their merits, or (in some part) because of their shortness.

Expressing a distrust of shorts publicly will be unseemly, unacceptable, a stature slur. To call attention to the inferior performance of the short group (it will be said) shows prejudice, a hidden antipathy for shorts. On the premise that the selection is known to have been deliberately diluted by the consideration of some physical characteristic, members of groups in whose favor that dilution was designed are inescapably suspect.

The individual talls displaced by such preferences (and all those who believed that they were so displaced) would harbor justifiable resentment, no doubt. But talls as a group would not suffer. Shorts as a group, on the other hand, would suffer mightily. Poorly prepared shorts, marginally qualified shorts who would not have been admitted if they were not short, would rarely fail to recognize their own unsuitability for the roles into which they have been thrust. The internal burden would be heavy. Their tall colleagues (or classmates or competitors or patients) reasonably presuming the part that shortness had played in their selection, would view them with silent disdain.

But all shorts, whatever the level of their actual talent, would find themselves under an intellectual cloud created by -- could it be? -- their height! Even when shorts perform extremely well that performance is likely to win less than full credit because it would be viewed, by talls and shorts alike, through a veil of doubt and lowered expectations. The known preference gives rational ground to conjecture, regarding each short, that she had been given favor because she was short; behind her back she is likely to be referred to (with a knowing look) as the short candidate. Any short individual appointed or admitted could never know, for sure, what accounted for her selection.

Short people may be thankful that all this is fantasy, that we have not done this terrible thing to them. Black students and black professionals have not been fortunate. Not height, but skin color, equally unrelated to intellectual excellence, has been transformed into onus. What would happen to shorts in this absurd thought experiment does happen in fact to blacks, to other minorities, and even to women, in institutions of all kinds.

Attending to the race of one who achieves distinction rather than to the talent and character resulting in that achievement often reveals hidden disdain. Anecdotes prove nothing, but here is one that illuminates the insult. A new president was appointed at Wayne State University in Detroit, in 1997. Here is the opening of the report of his appointment in one of the major Michigan newspapers:

> In a time when affirmative action is being criticized throughout the United States, Wayne State University has appointed its first African-American President. In December 1996, Wayne State's former President, David Adamany, announced his retirement.

Seven and a half months later, at an august public Board meeting, Irvin Reid was named the University's ninth president, making history by being the first black face among his eight predecessors. . . Wayne State Board of Governors Chair Denise Lewis said . . ."he's one of the leading African-Americans in higher education because he's been in high education for some 30 years."[23]

Is this not condescending, offensive? Is race preference good for President Reid and other distinguished black administrators? Individual members of a minority group may benefit from favors, but the minority as a whole is subverted by race preference. Invidious racial comparisons are invited. Stereotypes of racial inferiority are reinforced, given apparent substance by the preferential devices intended to give support to previously disadvantaged groups.

Had racists set out deliberately to besmirch minorities a more effective device could hardly have been chosen to exhibit their supposed inferiority. Persons preferred on grounds of race or ethnicity commonly perform poorly. This is not because they are minority members, but because of the method of their selection. If some demon had sought to concoct a scheme aimed at undermining the credentials of minority scholars, professionals and students, to stigmatize them permanently and humiliate them publicly, no more ingenious plan could have been devised that the system of preferences now defended as a social good.

Support for preferences among minorities themselves is nevertheless understandable. Each member of a group preferred may reasonably say to herself that the system is one in which I am myself a likely beneficiary. All naturally think chiefly of their own advantage; each is reasonable in hoping to gain such advantage, and is not at all foolish in supporting a system that, although it may injure the group as a whole over the long run, offers that individual the hope of substantial personal benefit. However bad a system of minority preference may be in the large, one who accepts its benefits within existing rules does no wrong.

Support for preference among ethnic minorities is reinforced by the advocacy of celebrated persons referred to as civil rights leaders, whose influence is enhanced by enlarging preferential programs. Designing preferences, advocating them and enforcing them, has become a cottage industry, well paid in money and prestige. The defense of preferences, and the claims of victimhood that are put forward to justify that defense, is a principal business of those who make their livelihood exploiting racial divisions.

Why do white advocates of preferential programs fail to see the damage they do to the minorities they aim to assist? Some contend that it is the feeling of guilt for the historical oppression of minorities that drives many whites to make what they suppose to be a form of restitution. One black scholar asserts that American institutions, when it comes to race, "are driven entirely by white guilt." Critical capacities are suspended, says he; the strategy is one of appeasement.[24]

Perhaps. But guilt feelings, however much or little justified, cannot account for obtuseness. The failure to acknowledge the damage done to minorities is chiefly explained, I submit, by the mistaken conviction that no real damage has been done.

The stigmatization of minorities by preference is not a threat, some say, because the greater frequency of poor performance among them will be overshadowed by the enormous variety of performance among students and professionals of every stripe. Racial disparities, it is thought, will go unnoticed. Objective differences in intellectual talent are not great, and are not reliably measurable. Because racial disparities will go unnoticed, so preferences will not have the adverse impact widely feared.

Wrong. Differences in the quality of work done cannot be long hidden; the disparity between the performance of those preferred and those not preferred becomes evident to all. The performance of any preferred group will be (statistically) inferior. When the preferred group is identified by color, that inferior performance will be linked in the public mind to the race of those preferred.

In the world of athletics, where performance is very public, race preference will not be tolerated. Sports teams play to win, caring little about their racial balance. Blacks constitute a high percentage of the players in the National Football League, and an even higher percentage in the National Basketball Association -- much higher than the percentage of blacks in the population at large. They are in those lineups because they are good, very good.

Suppose — here is another thought experiment -- it were decided that basketball teams must exhibit racial proportionality. Suppose some system had been devised to insure that, in every college and professional basketball game, the percentage of the races on the court must reflect the approximate racial proportions in the population at large. Substantial preference would have to be given to inferior white players, of course. Picture the scene as the teams take the floor: three or four whites are in the starting lineup of each team; black players known by all to be markedly superior to them remain on the bench. The relative mediocrity of the white players preferred is there for every eye to see. Put aside the unfairness to blacks whose deserved places are taken by preferred whites. What must the fans, the coaches, the players of all colors be thinking about the whites who play in that corrupted system? What will be assumed about the abilities of every additional white player who enters the game? If some white player is very good, yet stumbles, to what will his errors be attributed? What will be generally supposed to be the reason that white is out there playing?

This is fantasy, of course, because we feel no need to eliminate ethnic disparities on sports teams. The idea strikes us as absurd because the color of the players is not what counts; what counts is their skill. We want our teams to win. In elementary school the importance of winning may be minimized for good reason. But at the high school and college level, and certainly in the world of professional sports, winning is the object of game.

The case is no different in any field of serious work or study. In a hospital or a courtroom, where lives are at stake, success -- securing the health of the patient, the acquittal of the defendant -- is the overriding objective. We no more care whether the surgeon be black or the lawyer Hispanic than we care whether the quarterback is white. We are right not to care. Without preferences the percentage of minorities enrolled in the nation's law schools and medical schools would be lower than it now is. That is a regrettable consequence of the state of preparation of minority youngsters, just as their domination of some athletic teams is a consequence of their early training. We will not change the standards of performance on the basketball court to achieve racial balance there.. Ought we change the standards for performance in a hospital to achieve racial balance in its operating rooms? Where the work is important skin color is simply not relevant.

In the professions, forcing racial balance through preference is as counterproductive as it would be in professional sports. In the professions it is more harmful. Scientists, doctors, journalists, lawyers, do not fumble footballs or miss baskets on national TV. But human lives and fortunes rest in their hands, and those who blunder repeatedly are soon identified, if not by the public by their colleagues. When you and I are in serious need of professional help we seek the very best service we can find and afford; nothing could matter less than the ethnicity of the person we depend upon.

We do not for a moment think that there is no objective way judge the performance of the lawyers we hire, or the doctors who treat us. I teach logic; I can tell you with some precision who among my students have a solid grasp of the principles of correct reasoning, and who among them understand the material less well, or poorly. Intellectual strength and attainment is an objective matter. Judging it, like judging the skill of a quarterback, may not be quantitatively exact, but evaluations can be quite reliable. My colleagues in the University of Michigan hospitals make judgments of proficiency every bit as reliable as the judgments of our athletic coaches. Students well prepared for the intellectual rigors of veterinary medicine, or accountancy, or for graduate study in mathematics or philosophy, can be readily distinguished from those who are not. Skilled professionals can be readily identified. Intellectual talents -- the ability to master complex theoretical materials, to apply theory to complicated fact situations, to undertake careful analyses and make subtle distinctions -- are not harder to identify than talents on the athletic field. Where performance standards are high, the inability to perform effectively or compete successfully is generally ascertainable by those skilled in that activity. Race cannot make up for it.

Wherever intellectual weakness is found to accompany some external physical characteristic in disproportionate number -- as it must when some physical characteristic is given weight in the selection process -- the bearers of that characteristic become unavoidably suspect. The fact that some who possess that characteristic are also among the very best cannot ward off the natural inference associating that physical characteristic with inferiority. Preferential affirmative action, here in the United States and around the world, brands racial groups as inferior, inflicting upon the members of those groups the injury they least deserve to suffer. By thrusting minorities into positions in which their relative performance must prove statistically inferior, contemporary affirmative action gives maddening plausibility to the judgments that persons of some colors are not capable of meeting the standards of performance imposed on those of other colors.[25]

In that mythical world in which shorts are given preference over non-shorts in college admission, who is done greater injury: the class of talls among whom some are displaced by untalented but favored shorts? Or those shorts who would have won their places fairly through intellect and energy but who are nevertheless forever suspect because of their shortness? Many among affirmative action minorities need no preference, want none and get none, yet lose the respect of colleagues and clients who have good reason to suspect that their places had been won through race preference. Minority professionals who have not been preferred, whose intellect and character would have won them universal esteem without any regard for color, are seriously undermined by preference. No matter their industry, their talent, their hard-won attainments, they are seen to be black or brown and believed (by majority and minority members both, and perhaps even by themselves) to be where they are by virtue of a preference having nothing to do with their talents. Every minority member who excels is subverted; no member of the preferred minority can escape distrust.

Earlier I noted the bitter complaint of a fine black law student, MKF, about the affirmative action preferences at the University of Michigan Law Review. When minority students are interviewed by judges for clerkships, or by law firms for employment, they are not asked whether they took advantage of affirmative action preferences; that question cannot be asked without offense. But if in fact no such racial advantages have been received, how can that be made known? The resume cannot show that affirmative action preference had been declined. Doing that would be indiscreetly vain, and would indirectly harm others who did not decline them. That report, even when true, simply cannot be given. "We are as qualified as well-qualified whites, [MKF wrote] but nobody knows it, and, in fact, outsiders have a legitimate reason to doubt it."[26] The net of preference is inescapable.

Majority students who gain the prestigious editorships on law review, MKF notes with resentment, remain unimpeachable.[27] The preferential policy, he observes, is "motivated in part to soothe the consciences of those not subject to it."[28] But affirmative action in the form of preference

minimizes minority efforts and achievements. John McWhorter, a professor of linguistics at the University of California, writes:

"Affirmative Action in education denies black students the
incentives to do their very best. There is no such thing as a human being doing their very best when they are told they only
have to do pretty darn well. That will never raise a group to
parity with whites and Asians. That is my reason for not liking
Affirmative Action -- because it keeps black students down."[29]

Prof. McWhorter and MKF are unusually outspoken; high-achievers
among the minorities often find it difficult to be so candid. But the
unfairness and the damage done are real.

Prof. Stephen Carter, who became a senior professor at the Yale
Law School, reports what he calls the "best black" syndrome. He re-
counts his own experience after having won, as a youth, the "National
Achievement Scholarship" awarded to "outstanding Negro students."
The award he really wanted was the National Merit Scholarship, so he
inquired: If he accepted the former might he be considered for the latter? No. And must he decide on this right away? Yes, but no matter, he
was told: 'you wouldn't win a National Merit Scholarship anyway, ... the
people who get National Achievement Scholarships are never good
enough to get National Merit Scholarships.' Carter continues:

"I was stunned -- the more so when, later, a number of white
students with lower test scores than mine and similar grades
were awarded National Merit Scholarships. The lesson was
that the smartest students of color were not considered as capable as the smartest white students, and therefore would not
be allowed to compete with them, but only with each other.

"It is called the 'best black' syndrome, and all black people who
have done well in school are familiar with it. We are measured
by a different yardstick: first black, only black, best black. The

best black syndrome is cut from the same cloth as the implicit and demeaning tokenism that often accompanies racial preferences. 'Oh, we'll tolerate so-and-so on our faculty, because she's the best black.' Not because she's the best qualified candidate, but because she's the best qualified black candidate. She can fill the black slot. And then the rest of the slots can be filled in the usual way: with the best qualified candidates."[30]

Who is responsible for the creation and spread of this "best black" syndrome? No one knows better than Stephen Carter, who explains:

"This dichotomy between the 'best' and the 'best black' is not something manufactured by racists to denigrate the abilities of professionals who are not white. On the contrary, it is reinforced from time to time by those students who demand that universities commit to hiring some pre-set number of minority faculty members. What they are really saying is: 'Go out and hire the best blacks.' And it is further reinforced by faculty members who see these demands as nothing more than claims for simple justice.

"The best black syndrome creates in those of us who have benefited from racial preferences a peculiar contradiction. We know, because we are told over and over, that we are the best black people in our fields, whatever those fields may be.... At the same time we long for more. We yearn to be called what our achievements often deserve: simply the best -- no qualifiers needed!

"No, what I describe isn't racism, but it is in its way every bit as tragic. It is nearly as insulting. The best black? There are the best people -- that's one category -- and there are the best black people -- that's another. And those twain don't meet.

"Racial preferences [Carter concludes] must certainly reinforce the best black syndrome.... The best black syndrome is demeaning and oppressive and ought to be eradicated.... [but] in an era when so many doubt the talents of those of us who have benefited from preferences, 'best black' can be a substitute for 'best affirmative action baby.'[31]

Race preference is very bad for the minorities it purports to help.

End Notes -- Chapter 7

1   Details of the race preferences given at the University of Michigan became known because its admissions systems were the subject of prolonged federal litigation, concluding only in 2003. The two cases, initiated in 1997, are *Gratz v. Bollinger,* (539 U.S. 234), addressing preference in undergraduate admissions, and *Grutter v. Bollinger,* (539 U.S. 306) addressing preference given by the Michigan Law School. These cases are discussed more fully in reporting the impact of preference on American universities in the following chapter.

2   *The Journal of Blacks in Higher Education* has reported this evidence in much detail, in many issues from 1994 to the present.

3   Theodore Cross, "Minority Students in Medical Education: Facts and Figures," *The Journal of Blacks in Higher Education,* January 1993.

4   "What If There Was No Affirmative Action?" *The Journal of Blacks in Higher Education,* Spring, 1994.

5   *Ibid,* p. 47.

6   California Department of Education, *Working Together for the Education of All Students,* Sacramento, 1994. The standards referred to were those in force at that time, of course.

7   Race preferences at the University of Michigan are recounted in full detail in my book, *A Conflict of Principles: The Battle over Affirmative Action at The University of Michigan,* University Press of Kansas, 2014.

8   Memorandum from the Michigan Law Review Association, Ann Arbor. Michigan. April 3, 1992.

9   *Ibid.*

10 From an unpublished letter, in my files, written by MKF to the Editorial Board of the Michigan Law Review.

11 *Ibid.*

12 *Ibid.*

13 *The New York Times,* 25 May 1993.

14 *The Michigan Daily,* 21 October 1993.

15 *The New York Times,* 25 May 1993.

16 *The New York Times,* 7 June 1993.

17 *The New York Times,* 15 September 1991.

18 *Ibid.*

19 *Time Magazine,* 27 May 1991.

20 *The New York Times, 15* September 1991. Emphasis added.

21   *Insight,* 20 June 1994.

22   Reported by Troy Duster, a sociologist at the University of California, in *Time Magazine,* 27 May 1991.

23   *The Ann Arbor News,* August 1997.

24   See Shelby Steele, *A Dream Deferred: The Second Betrayal of Black Freedom in America.*

25   The process works also in reverse. Not long ago, the quota for Jewish students in some Ivy League universities (where they were distinctly unwelcome) was tiny; those who made the cut had to be exceedingly able. The myth of the Jews as super-smart was given support by the rational inference then that any Jew enrolled at Harvard, or Columbia, must indeed have been very brainy.

26   MKF, in his letter.

27   *Ibid.* It will be recalled that MKF, a member of the editorial Board who had himself received no preference, was writing to his fellow members who planned to give preference.

28   MKF, in his letter.

29   John McWhorter, in an interview with Lee Hubbard on 10 January 2002, reported online in *African.com.* Prof. McWhorter's critique is presented and defended at length in his 2001 book, *Losing the Race.*

30   Stephen L. Carter, "The Best Black, and Other Tales," *Reconstruction,* Vol. I, No. I, winter 1990, p. 7. This account reappears in Carter's 1991 book: *Reflections of an Affirmative Action Baby.*

31   Reflections of an Affirmative Action Baby.

CHAPTER 8

Race Preference is Bad for Universities

Race preference is bad for everyone. Its worst consequences befall the racial minorities preferred. But also in colleges and universities, where such preference is pervasive, the consequences have been dreadful. The intellectual impact there is fundamental; the moral impact is pernicious.

The quest for intellectual excellence is the mark of fine universities. In them devotion to truth and to high standards is genuine. Race preference lowers intellectual standards inescapably however because, when race has become a consideration in admission or appointment intellectual considerations are necessarily diluted. It is not politically feasible for educational institutions to acknowledge that they have done this to themselves. Committed to race preference yet devoted to intellect, the universities are trapped between a rock and a whirlpool. Inadmissible realities must be disguised or denied. Unwilling to cleanse themselves of race preference, they are caught up in hypocrisy and duplicity.

Commitment to the principle of equal treatment is ardently professed. University officers affirm explicitly that they will tolerate no discrimination by race or creed or sex; admission and employment in the university must be non-discriminatory. They mean it — yet even as they say it they treat students and faculty of different races differently. The stark inconsistency between what they urge and what they do cannot be confessed, even to themselves, and even when the duplicity has become widely obvious. So our universities have become saturated with dishonesty. Where devotion to principle is taught, principles are betrayed wholesale. The contrast between what is professed and what is practiced is appalling.[1]

We are guided (they say) by the striving for excellence; our faculty and our students must meet the highest intellectual standards. For decades in America's premier universities this has simply not been true. Standards have been deliberately lowered because only by lowering standards could the number of minority students enrolled, and the number of minority faculty appointed, come close to satisfying self-imposed affirmative action goals.

As the detail of these consequences unfold below, bear this in mind: There is no inconsistency between membership in any ethnic minority and the highest intellectual attainment. This truth should be spelled out in letters so large that he who runs may read. Blacks, Hispanics, Native Americans, exhibit every excellence of humankind, as do members of all ethnic and racial groups. The lowering of standards obliged by preferential affirmative action is not the consequence of the intellectual inferiority of the groups favored.

Then why does race preference have that outcome? Because the number of minority members affirmative action demands (whether as 'goal' or as 'quota' or as 'target'), is far greater than the number of intellectually qualified minorities available to satisfy that demand. Whatever the reasons for this, it is a fact. The imbalance between the supply of minority scholars and the demand for them is a reality that no special admissions program or opportunity hiring program can change.

The implicit supposition of preferential programs has been that forcing racial proportionality will somehow overcome that imbalance. Not so. Ethnic proportionality has been the explicit objective of the universities for years.[2] But obliging ethnic ratios in the universities to mirror the ratios in the population at large cannot alter the capacities of the persons applying, admitted, or hired. The demand for well-qualified minority scholars continues to exceed the supply. Until that supply is increased the demand can be satisfied only by lowering established standards. There is no other way to get the immediate results insisted upon. College administrators declare that standards are not being lowered, but no one with open eyes believes them. The evidence is irrefutable.[3]

The duplicity — in some cases the downright dishonesty — of university admissions officers was long difficult to document because access to the detailed mechanics of their preferential programs was tightly restricted to the inner circle.[4] Disclosure of the facts, it was feared, would trigger a barrage of litigation. At the Universities of Michigan, and Georgia, and Texas, the release of those documents has at last been forced, first by the use of the Freedom of Information Act, and then by the process of discovery in civil litigation. Before that release preferential policies were described in language whose object was to convince the public that double standards were not being applied, while applying them. With the veil of secrecy penetrated we learn how great institutions have abased themselves in the name of affirmative action"[5]

The first line of defense by college administrators is the insistence that in their institution unqualified students are never admitted. This is true, but only in the trivial sense that, since they themselves determine who is 'qualified,' all whom they admit are qualified; to be admitted by them is to be qualified. But if by 'qualified' is meant the exhibition of intellectual attainments that have traditionally served as the prerequisites for admission to scholarly institutions, the claim is false. The intellectual level of many who are admitted preferentially to reach racial goals is scandalous.

The second line of defense is a statistical deceit. "The average grade point level of our admitted students, affirmative action admittees included, has gone up, not down. Doesn't this prove that our preferences have not resulted in lowered standards?" No, it does not. Averaging the records of those admitted hides their full intellectual profile. The splendid records of some obscure the dismal records of those preferentially admitted. Intellectual selectivity for non-minority students increases, so the averages go up.

Averages cannot reveal the range of the numbers averaged; they hide the fact that lowered admission standards have been applied to some. The grade point averages and test scores required of those preferentially admitted are, in fact, markedly lower than those required of standard applicants.[6] At the select colleges and universities of our country there is a deliberately contrived set of double standards, devised to give and to hide preference by race.

The third line of defense is a verbal deceit: Admission is a complicated business and rightly depends upon much more than test scores and grades. Numerical criteria are therefore held to be misleading. This response is deceptive. Factors other than grades and scores do enter every admission decision, but it does not follow that there are no numerical standards in use. Quantitative factors are weighed differently for minority applicants. Public service, valiant efforts, and other marks of fine character are said to provide the rationale for the admission of minority applicants whose academic records are plainly deficient. But for white male applicants whose scores are low, fine character will be of little help. Administrative discretion gives unacknowledged preference by race. Leadership, determination, overcoming adversity may be rightly considered by admissions officers. Such virtues of character, however, are not more common or more notable among the racial groups preferred than they are among Asians and whites. The consideration of character and other subjective factors has the result of favoring minority applicants because such factors are introduced and used in considering admission for some but not for others.

Lower standards are defended with a fourth argument, the claim that judgments of intellectual merit and potential cannot be objectively made. High scores do not insure success; bad grades often do not lead to continued failure. Anecdotes of ill-prepared minority applicants who prove successful, of whom there are many, are offered as evidence. To infer from such anecdotes that there can be no objectivity in intellectual judgment is false. Reliable judgments of achievement and promise are commonly made and must be made. No predictive system is wholly reliable, of course. There will always be some who overcome dreadful beginnings, and some who fail to realize great promise. But on the whole we make reasonably accurate judgments among those who apply for admission regarding who among them are most likely to succeed, and who most likely to fail.

Colleges and professional schools are constantly appraising the intellectual potential of their applicants; the tone and atmosphere of an institution is set by the quality of the students admitted. The surest way to judge the intellectual quality of a college is to examine the intellectual profile of its students. The ability to make such judgments reliably is precisely what accounts for the ratings of premier institutions like Stanford and the University of Chicago. They enroll the students who, at the time of their application, are known to exhibit enormous potential; colleges and community colleges of the second and third tier are obliged to enroll applicants who may be fairly described as less distinguished. Some in that latter category will prove themselves marvelously in the end, true enough, but that does not begin to show that objective judgments of merit cannot be made.

Three measures are almost universally relied upon in some degree by the admissions offices of universities: 1) the applicant's grade point average in previous schooling, with performance in more difficult substantive materials given greater weight; 2) the applicant's rank in class in the secondary school (or in the undergraduate college, for professional school applications), where the standards of that previous school are also taken into account; and 3) the applicant's performance on some standardized test, like the SAT or the LSAT (Law School Admission Test), or the ACT or the MCAT (Medical College Admission Test). Differing weights will be given to these intellectual factors, but one or more of them will play a central role in the admissions systems of all respectable colleges.[7]

These instruments have been quite finely honed over the years; their reliability and validity have been repeatedly tested and are well established. The strongest applicants for admission, those with greatest potential, can be identified, to serve the scholarly purposes of an institution. To the extent that they are subordinated to non-intellectual considerations the admission process is corrupted, politicized. Every dilution of intellectual measure drives the enrolled student population toward mediocrity. This applies not only to dilution by race. The "dumb jock" is not a myth but a reality; so much preference is given for athletic talent that a varsity athlete with a B+ average is viewed an intellectual star. But the irrelevant consideration that has most corrupted admissions in recent years is race.

The percentage of minority students who perform with excellence on those objective intellectual measures is substantially lower than the percentage of minority students in the population at large. This is certainly not -- I repeat -- because race is a mark of inferiority. But the statistical reality must be confronted. To overcome that reality the advocates of preference use two devices; the first is an attack upon the reliability of standard examinations, the second is a deliberately misleading technique for the reporting of exam performance.

Tests like the widely used SAT[8] are first attacked as 'culturally biased.' Consistently poorer performance by Hispanic and black students on these examinations, it is claimed, is simply a consequence of the cultural distortion and prejudice built into the tests themselves. Racially disparate results may be accounted for (it is claimed) by the peculiarities of the tests. The unsoundness of this argument has been repeatedly established by exhaustive scientific inquiry; we know with virtual certainty that it is not cultural bias in the testing that causes those unhappy racial disparities. Cultural distortion long ago became a concern of testing services, and was long ago eliminated from the standardized exams now used for college admissions. Bias imposed by the tests plays no role in determining the level of performance of ethnic groups; that tired claim is simply unwarranted.

Any admissions test is biased if it systematically predicts unfairly how some group will perform after being enrolled. The SAT does not mispredict; it is, in fact, all too accurate in its predictions. Asians and whites score substantially higher than Hispanics and blacks — and the former groups regularly outperform the latter in college too. Racially disparate test results are painful, but the problem does not lie with the test.

In fact the reverse is true. Independent scholars of fair testing agree that carefully constructed and well-validated scholastic aptitude tests are among the very best instruments for making reliable judgments of intellectual promise. The SAT has been scientifically appraised; it predicts the future performance of minority students even better than that of majority students. But it does slightly over-predict, not under-predict, the subsequent performance of minority students. If there is any bias in the SAT it favors minority applicants who take that test.[9] Objective measurements of the intellectual promise of college applicants cannot be evaded by blaming the racially disparate results on the testing instruments.

Standardized tests play a far smaller role in admissions than do the grade point averages of students in their previous schooling. Since these averages of academic performance over several years also reveal racial disparities, they also must be evaded. "Racial norming" is one device used to this. The manipulative principle is simple: If, for purposes of report, we separate applicants into racially discrete classes, we can report the standing of any member of a given group in relation only to other members of that group. If we are told, for example, that the performance of a minority applicant is at the 81st percentile (in the top fifth) of applicants, we would infer that she is a desirable candidate. But that inference will be unwarranted if the scores have been race-normed, since that number will then indicate only the top fifth of minority applicants; among all applicants the applicant may actually place in the bottom fifth. By reporting the records of minority applicants using only comparisons to the records of other minority applicants, those records are made to appear far better than they really are.

Why do such deceptions multiply? Administrators need them if affirmative action goals are to be met. The resort to race-norming illuminates the fundamental problem: without lowering standards there is no way to achieve the number of minorities called for by ethnic proportionality. First attack the intellectual measures themselves. If that is shown to be a case of shooting the messenger because of his message, statistical chicanery may do the trick. Institutions determined to give race preference in the name of affirmative action must, one way or another, lower their standards. There is no escaping this need to do it, and the equally compelling need to hide the fact that it is being done.

Another widespread evasion takes the form of simply rejecting quantified student records. No numerical system can yield satisfactory results because only individualized attention to the entire record of the applicant, considered "holistically," can yield useful results. But individualization, often wise when it is feasible, must also be free of racial discrimination. If applicants with poor grades and low test scores are admitted because they have overcome great adversity, or because they manifest unusual enthusiasm, such considerations must be weighed for all applicants without regard to their race. This is given lip service, but the whole point of the current enthusiasm for the "individualization" of admissions in select universities is the need to find ways in which race preference can be given backhandedly.

At the University of California, in spite of the constitutional prohibition of race preference in that state,[10] the admission system has been altered so as to replace objective examinations with subjective evaluations, permitting very wide administrative discretion. The aim is patently preferential. The so-called "comprehensive review" of applicants, in which objective criteria are minimized, and the special life circumstances of the applicant are weighed, formerly used for only a fraction of those admitted, is now applied to all applicants. The public justification for the change was "outreach" — but no one seriously doubts that the change was designed to make possible, by the exercise of administrative discretion, more minority admissions than normal academic review would produce. Academic performance is now only one of three requirements for admission to the University of California. The others are designedly subjective, including the degree to which the applicant has successfully met "life challenges" such as the ability to "overcome adversity." What cannot be done openly is done under the table.

Lowering standards has long proved effective in reducing the numbers of some disfavored group. At the universities of the Ivy League some decades ago the disfavored applicants were not Asians and whites (as at the University of California today) but Jews, who did too well on the College Board exams used for admission. To exclude the Jews while retaining the exams would exhibit unseemly bigotry. They adopted instead the same course adopted by the University of California today; they replaced the examinations that gave the wrong results with the evaluation of character. Yale and Princeton and other universities announced -- to cope with what they frankly called "the Hebrew problem" — that in the places of those high-performing Jewish test-takers they would enroll more "well rounded" students of good character. Harvard President A. Lawrence Lowell wrote that admissions decisions should be based on "a personal estimate of character on the part of the Admissions authorities."[11] Former President of the University of California Richard Atkinson sought to eliminate the SATs for similar reasons, he replaced Lowell's "well-rounded" with the code word "holistic." Harvard successfully reduced the number of most of its Jews in the 1930s; California struggles to reduce the numbers of its high-scoring Asians and whites today. When disfavored groups do too well on entrance exams it is convenient to eliminate the exams, or at least to greatly reduce their role.

Admitting some preferred students on a lower standard (apart from its adverse impact on the students displaced, and apart from the injury done to the minorities preferred) damages the university. The intellectual quality of students enrolled is the principal support of most intellectual activity in the university. It is as important as the quality of the faculty. Learning in classrooms, discovery in laboratories, depth and excitement in seminars, all depend upon intellectually talented students. Extracurricular activities and the spirit of the institution also depend upon that talent. Debates, lectures and discussions in residence halls, exchanges in the commons rooms, the feeling of intellectual seriousness in and out of classrooms -- almost everything important in the atmosphere of a good university is determined by the quality of the students admitted. Fine students demand a fine faculty, bring out the best in their instructors and in their fellow students. They make the university. Those who have taught or studied in a fine university will testify that nothing contributes more to its excellence than the intellectual capacity and achievements of its students.

The impact of lowering the intellectual quality of entering students has been illustrated vividly in the recent history of CCNY, the City College of New York, now one member of a family of colleges constituting the City University of New York (CUNY). City College was one of America's premier centers of learning for generations; its students were poor and disadvantaged, many were the children of recent immigrants -- but they were able and they were determined to succeed.The standards at CCNY in those days were very high; its graduates won international acclaim, many Nobel Prizes. Called "the poor man's Harvard" it really surpassed Harvard intellectually because at CCNY distinction was never diluted by money or by family. If you couldn't cut it you didn't stay.

But political pressures could not be resisted. High standards for admission were replaced by a system of "open admissions" -- and CCNY sank speedily from distinction to mediocrity. In the newly transformed City College many students were nearly illiterate. Occasional success stories only highlighted the generally depressed level of intellectual activity there.[12] Much of the teaching that went on at City College became remedial; that was essential because ill-prepared students once admitted must be brought to a level at which they can begin to do college work. Courses at high school level, even some at junior high school level, were offered. Students were admitted with academic records so poor that their chances of real college success were virtually nil.The result was intense dissatisfaction among the faculty, many of the best of them soon departed.The reputation of CCNY as the home of brilliant students and distinguished scholars had been thrown away.[13]

That painful history is an extreme manifestation of a process that goes on wherever admission standards are significantly reduced. It is going on now in many once great centers of learning. Few have sunk so far as CCNY did. But when students who would not normally have been admitted are enrolled because of their race, the path of the institution is downward.The large-scale failure of preferentially admitted students would be humiliating, and politically intolerable. Remedial instruction for those who ought not to have been admitted in the first place has therefore become common a feature of American university life. Where racial targets require the deepest preference, the burden of remediation (detested by serious scholars) is often the heaviest.

Courses designed to teach ill-educated underclassmen how to write grammatically correct English have multiplied. Adjunctive centers are established to help ill-prepared students learn how to organize their thoughts, construct a paragraph, write an essay. Professors meet to devise ways to teach students how to study, how to draw inferences, how to take notes, how to identify the main idea in a written passage -- all skills formerly mastered in junior high school. Medical schools, where race preference is common, appoint remedial tutors with euphemistic names to supply affirmative action students with the basic tools of biology and chemistry. What were formerly requirements for admission to medical school can be retained as requirements no longer, because the enrollment of the targeted number of ethnic minorities is made impossible by their retention. "Mentoring programs" have become common, in which students deficient in the most basic skills are assigned to individual faculty members for guidance. Demands for special support proliferate; the academic counseling staffs in large universities have grown huge. There arise separate "minority counseling offices" to tutor, to pull, or to push students who would not have been enrolled but for their ethnicity. Preferential admissions absorb ever-greater portions of the time and energy of college faculties.[14]

None of this comes cheap. While the number of enrolled students in colleges declines, the number of administrators on the staff on the American universities increases dramatically. Most of the new administrators contribute nothing to the teaching and research functions of the university; they are hired mainly to support students who ought never to have been admitted. Counseling offices, tutoring centers, financial aid and loan offices, performance monitors, each with its complement of managers and assistant managers, consume great chunks of college resources. An "affirmative action" bureaucracy emerges in every university; new remedial and race-oriented programs are created, more staff is called for to manage and monitor those programs. Students of different colors and ethnicities must be enrolled in race-oriented clubs and organizations; separate counselors will be needed for each ethnicity, and often separate facilities as well. Tensions arise among competing minorities and these must be addressed with "workshops- in "diversity management" conducted by "experts" in "multicultural relations" who helped to create the problems they are asked to solve. Ethnic data must be compiled, but only the analysis of such data can justify their collection. Reports are prepared, almost invariably calling for greater representation of underrepresented minorities in the col- lege, and for the appointment of more staff who can put newly enrolled minority students at ease. These reports are sent from one level of the bureaucracy to the next for discussion and implementation. Minority goals must be established and affirmative action plans devised to reach them; these must be reviewed and revised and then implemented (with uncertain success) through preferences administered by sub-sections of the admissions and employment offices. Implementation in every unit must be continually reassessed, and every assessment is likely to produce additional reports charting numerical progress and calling for new initiatives. Task forces are established to overcome "the gap" — the disparity in the performance of racial groups. Self-congratulatory booklets and newsletters are distributed to alumni and the press. These will commonly conclude by lamenting the great distance yet to be traversed before racial balance is achieved, and by observing that the racial goals can be achieved only increased funding for "di- versity programs" and new minority staff.[15] Most of this is without serious intellectual merit. The overall damage done to our universities by the morass of the affirmative action establishment is impossible to calculate.

It was all to be temporary, we were told. Preferences would be needed at first, but once achieved diversity would be self-sustaining. Students preferentially admitted would be quickly "brought up to speed." — or, old-fashioned standards abandoned, their "speed" will no longer be measured. But the transience of preference was a delusion. Racial balance being the objective, all the machinery of preference is solidi- fied and protected until it is achieved, and once achieved, is retained to safeguard that balance. Bloated administrations are overseen by government agencies largely staffed by members of the very groups preferred. Few press for the deflation of the bureaucracy because doing so is likely to be condemned as evidence of "institutional racism." University preferences never shrink.[16]

Well-meaning students in the white majority, pressing for preference as an instrument of justice, have learned how to cow college administrators. Their demands are likely to include the creation of a new ethnic studies unit, requiring more minority faculty, or the appointment of a new affirmative action administrator with more staff, and so on. The costs of complying with such demands can be hidden in a complicated budget; resistance to them may lead to disorder. The affirmative action bureaucracy thrives.

The higher the minority racial targets the more difficult it is to reach them, and the more necessary to lower standards for admission. This increases the need for remedial support, and for monitoring to insure compliance. Admissions officers, department heads, deans, even presidents apologize for past failure to meet affirmative action goals, and follow that apology with promises of renewed efforts to 'do better.' Racial proportionality is the target, first in enrollment, eventually in graduation.[17]

Most of this escapes public notice. Documentary evidence is kept secret; discretionary devices giving preference are nearly undetectable. But on occasion the cat gets out of the bag. Three such exposures I report briefly below; they are the tip of the iceberg.

A) Admissions preferences given by the law school of Georgetown University, in Washington DC, were discovered by a student editor of the *Law Weekly*, Timothy Maguire, who had been working in the admissions office. Maguire was vilified by the Dean of the Law School when the details of those admission practices became public, and efforts were made to expel him. All copies of the issue of *Law Weekly* in which the facts were revealed were confiscated. The Dean asserted that the consideration of race was no part of the Law School admission policy. The truth of that statement may be judged in the light of the published facts:

The average Law School Admission Test score of all enrolled students at Georgetown Law School that year was 43; the average LSAT score of all enrolled black students was 36. To be considered for admission at Georgetown, white applicants needed to be in the top 15% of all those taking the LSAT score that year; but black applicants in the top 40% were told they had "a strong chance of acceptance." The grade point average of white students enrolled was 3.7 (just below A); the grade point average of black students enrolled was 3.2 (just above B).

The Dean announced that admission policies ought not be publicly discussed because doing so might cause people to judge individual members of the benefited groups inappropriately. Standard academic responses were then repeated: All students at Georgetown "are qualified to meet the standards to graduate." Grade point averages at the school had risen since affirmative action had been introduced. The Law School, said the Dean, was sorely embarrassed by this "very painful event." The pain, one may infer, arose not from the reality of the preferences but from their disclosure.

B) The race preferences at the Law School of the University of Michigan were found to be yet more pronounced, their details exposed in a federal court trial, at which the University was obliged to defend itself against the suit of a 43-year old white woman with a superb record who claimed that the racial skewing of the admission system under which she had been rejected violated the law and the Constitution. Hundreds of pages of evidence were submitted to the Court at trial. A few of the facts disclosed will convey the spirit of what was going on there. Competition for admission there was and remains intense.

In one typical year applicants with good (B+) undergraduate records and very good LSAT scores (156-163) had less than a 3% chance of admission (7 of 238) if they were "Caucasian-Americans." But of African American applicants with identical grades and scores, 100% (17 of 17) were admitted.[18]

The "odds ratio" for admission is calculated to measure the extent of race preference. An odds ratio greater than 1 of one group to another indicates the greater likelihood of admission by an applicant from that group being admitted.[19] To put the numbers in perspective, the goal of medical investigations is to find a drug that may double or triple the odds of cure, relative odds of 2 or 3 to 1 is highly prized. An odds ratio greater than 100 is unheard of, and would be utterly astounding. In competing for admission to the Law School of the University of Michigan over the six years 1995-2000, the odds ratio for the admission of African American applicants compared to that of "Caucasian American" applicants was -- hold your hat -- 234! For the year 2000 by itself, the odds ratio was 443! Whatever the chances for admission were of a white applicant with a given set of credentials, a black applicant with the identical credentials that year had chances of admission *four hundred and forty three times as great.*[20]

Selective law schools — Georgetown, Michigan, Wisconsin, Harvard give enormous admission preference by race because they cannot meet their enrollment targets for minority students if they do not. There simply are not enough minority students around the country who can be admitted on the normal admission criteria. The year of the Georgetown exposure, 1990/91, the highest possible score on the Law School Admission Test (LSAT) was 48, and the average score of those admitted to Georgetown was 43; at the Michigan and Harvard and Chicago law schools it would have been higher. But in the law schools of the historically black universities around the country, the number of students at that level was very small. At Howard and Morehouse Universities, of all those taking the LSAT that year, more than half were in the bottom 10% of all takers nationwide, having scores between 0 and 19. At Hampton University 61%, at Jackson State College 74%, and at Grambling University 84% of those taking the LSAT had scores between 0 and 19. The pool of black applicants certainly contains some of the very finest applicants in the country. But it does not contain a sufficient number of excellent applicants to provide the select law schools with the number of black students they are determined to enroll. Those racial objectives can be met only by admitting minority students whose records are greatly inferior to those of applicants admitted without regard to race. Standards are sacrificed to achieve racial numbers. This is the price that race preference exacts.

C) Among applicants to undergraduate colleges the number of outstanding black candidates is far greater; but in that arena the competition for them, among select colleges, is greater still. Demand again far exceeds supply. Any black high school student with a good academic record and good SAT scores is likely to receive offers of four-year scholarships from several fine colleges, all tuition and expenses paid. Well-endowed universities can afford to pay for "diversity" with cash. But no money price can increase the supply. Affirmative action targets cannot be achieved with standards intact.

At those well-endowed universities superbly qualified white students compete desperately, often unsuccessfully, for admission. Full scholarships for non-minority students are rare. If admitted many will drain their family's resources. This racial contrast among applicants is the product of the aggressive quest by competing universities to enroll the few minority students who are well qualified on normal standards.

In the State of California all preference by race is now forbidden by Article 1, Section 31, of the State constitution.[21] Prior to its adoption Californians had extensive familiarity with the race preference they eventually voted to forbid. The experience of the University of California during the 1980s when race preference was rampant there is now being replicated in other states; that experience is worthy of brief reflection.[22]

When the Chancellor of the Berkeley campus of the University of California resigned in 1990 he announced that his proudest achievement had been the racial diversification of the freshman class there, adding: "These achievements are not at the expense of quality, as some have claimed." Not true; they were at the expense of quality, and this is proved by the data, of which some samples follow.

Efforts to narrow the academic gap between minority and non-minority high school graduates had long had little success. The California Department of Education put the facts (in 1994) bluntly: "The mean academic scores of blacks are so low that fewer than 5% of black students have the grades necessary to enter the University of California system."[23] They did enter the UC system in great numbers, however, because affirmative action required it. By the mid-90s, blacks were overrepresented at UC Berkeley by 40%, Hispanics overrepresented by 10%, and whites under represented by 47%.

How was this possible? Only by adjusting the criteria for "qualification." For Asians and whites admitted to Berkeley during 1987 and 1988 the average SAT score was 1270 (of a possible 1600); the average SAT score for Hispanics was 1037, and for blacks the average score was 979. The group differences are huge, roughly equivalent to a four-year gap in academic preparation and achievement. As the number of whites admitted decreased the intellectual selectivity for that group increased — and the gap between the two racial groups grew wider. Academic standards for white and Asian applicants at Berkeley rose (because of competition among them for a declining, number of places) and the overall SAT averages of the entering classes were thus maintained. But the entering classes at UC Berkeley came to consist of two distinct components, one of whites and Asians whose records were outstanding, the other of Hispanics, African Americans and Native

Americans whose records were markedly inferior. Race preference at Berkeley "produced two student populations whose academic levels barely overlap."[24]

An internal document at the University of California from that period revealed the facts. Three categories of students were distinguished: those admitted through "affirmative action," those admitted by "special action" (discretionary devices for enrolling athletes and additional minority students), and those admitted on the basis of their "academic index scores," a combination of intellectual factors constituting the normal entrance requirements. Of the thousands of students newly enrolled in 1987, for example, the number of African American students admitted on the basis of academic index was 1, the number of Native Americans 4, and the number of Hispanics 27. But of the entire entering class that year, 12% were black, 17% Hispanic. The Chancellor announced in 1990 that the standards for undergraduate admission at California had not been lowered. That was not true.

Things have changed in California. But there are fifty states, and more than three thousand colleges and universities in our country. Nearly all of them have committed themselves to increasing the number of blacks and other minorities enrolled, if necessary by giving race preference. Minority students with records that might normally qualify for admission to a good university are quickly soaked up by a tiny number of elite schools to which splendid scholarships are awarded. What are the rest to do? Consider the arithmetic:

Among the many thousands of college-bound black high school seniors registered for the Admissions Testing Program, there were, in 1983, only 66 with verbal SAT scores over 699 (out of a possible 800). Black seniors with math SAT scores over 699 numbered 205. The racial gap has grown yet wider. With verbal SAT scores of 600 white applicants have little chance of admission to a fine university; black students scoring at that level or above numbered less than one thousand,

and less than two thousand in the math SATs. Evenly distributed that would provide one or two moderately qualified black applicants for every three colleges in the country. The shortage of qualified minority applicants is severe; the competition for them, by the finest colleges, has become frenetic.[25]

Having gone to extraordinary lengths to recruit minority students, and to find them admissible, and to support them financially, the universities simply cannot allow them to wash out in great numbers; that would be callous and unproductive. If they are good enough to enroll, the thinking goes, they must be good enough to graduate. And so, as we have seen, special academic support services are established, special counselors appointed, special tutors provided. Still parity in graduation rates is not achieved. The institution must somehow be at fault; "institutional racism" must be the culprit — although what that means and how it is to be extirpated no one can clearly say.

If preferentially admitted students are to be graduated in proportional numbers, the corruption of the admissions process must be extended to the college curriculum itself. This is done in a variety of ways. First, the burden of normal academic requirements is eased; intellectually challenging requirements -- a sequence in chemistry, courses in a foreign language -- are waived for students in special need. Should race preference appear too obvious, the onerous requirements are simply eliminated for all. Mastery of a second language remains a requirement in very few fine colleges; even doctoral studies now commonly dispense with that requirement. The intellectual achievements required for graduation from most American universities today amount to something much less than admission to them entailed a century ago.

Some requirements remain, however, and within them there are courses that may prove difficult, so dispensation is given to students whose learning needs must be accommodated. Courses failed may be repeated, or final exams retaken, until a passing grade is received. Examinations failed may be given again, and again — and yet again, until a passing grade is obtained. To give such privileges to African-Americans and Hispanics but not to others would be unacceptable, so all students must be given the opportunity to re-take exams. In professional schools, and in the medical schools especially, students must prove themselves repeatedly and consistently irresponsible in order to flunk out.

A lifting of grade point averages is also achieved by offering special courses, populated largely by minority students and athletes, in assorted ethnic studies departments: black studies, Chicano studies, and so on -- in which classroom activity consists largely of the informal discussion of victimhood, and the grades, as might be expected, are uniformly splendid.

One black applicant to the Georgetown Law School with a very poor LSAT score had a grade point average so high that Timothy Maguire, reviewing the records of applicants there, checked her undergraduate transcript. Maguire wrote, "There, alongside a C+ in Shakespeare, a C in Economics, and an F in calculus, were 8 A's in African American courses."[26] That's only one case, of course.

The corruption infects individuals. Faculty members internalize the spirit of race preference in evaluating student work, and thus become complicit. Judgments at the margin are nudged to favor minority students whose failure would be embarrassing. The following true account, reported to me by a former member of the University of Michigan faculty, is illustrative: A failing grade was given to a minority student who had done very poor work in his course. The student complained, insisting that the examinations given did not adequately reflect his understanding of the material, and that he (the student) had been (he claimed) burdened with especially high expectations because of his race. Aware that there would be an ugly scene if those groundless charges were made publicly, the professor discussed the matter with the chairman of his department. Sympathetic but not helpful, the chairman said essentially this: 'You can stick to your guns, which would be just but will result in a terrible mess for our department -- or you can make a minor change in the student's grade, easily justifiable and of little consequence. Your call.' This professor wrote me: "I am ashamed to admit what I did. I avoided the mess and changed the grade." Again, only a single case.

A little extra generosity, faculty members may say to themselves, won't cause the heavens to fall. Excuses are made for inferior work; standards go down, grades go up. It is too painful to apply normal intellectual standards to the work of students who ought not to have been admitted in the first place.

Some faculty members rebel, even at great cost. A professor of mathematics at Temple University, Martin Eisen, to screen out students unable to do the work in his intermediate math courses, administered a pretest in 2001. The questions on that test were at junior high school level. For example: $(-10 + 4)$ = what?; Solve for x the following: $7x = 28$; $x+7 = 13$; $2x-3 = 15$. None of his freshman students could pass this 7th grade algebra test. Less than half of them could do simple arithmetic. The disparate impact of his pretest was so troubling that university administrators unilaterally changed the grades he had assigned -- and he was relieved of his duties by the President of the University.[27]

The fewer the categories distinguished on which college work is evaluated, the less need there will be for invidious intellectual comparisons. Levels of performance are collapsed into three: honors, pass, and fail. Virtually no one fails. Said one of Prof. Eisen's colleagues at Temple: "I'm teaching kids who should not be in college, but I can't fail them." The distinction between pass and honors becomes invidious in turn; where preference is given at one end of the scale, at the other end, and in the middle, almost everyone winds up an honors student. At Harvard, in 2001, it was revealed that 91% of all students had recently graduated "with honors."

To avoid having to give bad grades to students admitted preferentially the surest way of all is to avoid giving grades altogether. Grades cause embarrassment and create a competitive atmosphere in which minority students are uncomfortable and do not thrive. So evaluation is reduced to simply credit/no credit — and everyone enrolled gets credit, of course. Sometimes grades are retained, but if there is pressure to give better grades to some students than their work deserves, the grades of all other students must be raised as well. Everyone gets an A. Well, not quite everyone. At Harvard in 1996 only 46% of the grades given were A. Grading in many colleges has become a bad joke.[28] Preference entails lowered standards.

The lowering affects faculty standards also. The pressure in faculty appointments is downward because, in this case as in the other, the numbers of minorities sought cannot be obtained if high standards are retained. The President of Xavier University (an institution historically black) was criticized by some of the students there because too many of the newly appointed faculty were white. But Xavier's president was hard-pressed to find qualified black professors: "We're doing everything possible to increase the number of minority and African-American faculty. The clamor is going to be for more. But where are they going to come from?"[29]

More pressure does not solve this problem; it merely intensifies the competition for the few who are qualified. In the liberal arts -- English, mathematics, philosophy, and so on -- a doctorate is the normal prerequisite for a faculty appointment. Approximately 16,000 doctoral degrees are awarded in these fields each year to U.S. citizens. Of these, the number awarded to American blacks has been under 400, or less than 3%.[30] In some academic fields: astronomy, botany, classics, comparative literature, European history, geography, Russian, Italian, Chinese, and Arabic language and literature there was (in the year 1988, for example) not one single black Ph.D. in the entire country. In mathematics and computer science that year there were 2, out of a total of more than 600; in earth, atmospheric and marine sciences there were another 2. Even in American history the number of recent black Ph.Ds is countable on one's fingers. Abigail Thernstrom remarks: "Students and concerned faculty often argue that schools that really care will at the minimum employ a black scholar to teach Afro-American history. Where will they find them?"[31]

Research universities make extraordinary efforts to increase the flow of black Ph.Ds, and thus enlarge the pool for faculty appointments. Minority graduate students receive generous welcome and support, often including paid tuition and substantial stipend. But most black and Hispanic graduates with fine records then choose careers in professions more lucrative and more prestigious than the professoriat. The overall result is that the supply of qualified minority faculty remains small.

Frustrated by that reality, zealots insist that the number of black faculty simply must be increased. The University of Wisconsin adopted a five-year plan (in 1988) to increase minority faculty by 75%. Duke University pledged to add one minority faculty member to every department by 1993.[32] The state legislature imposed a minority quota of 30% of all new faculty in the community colleges of California, so "affirmative action job fairs" were held to meet the quota. Yale, Wellesley, Michigan, and other colleges and universities public announce their determination to increase the number of minority faculty. Most of these competitors must fail. When it appears that a distinguished minority scholar may be pried loose from his or her institution the bidding war that ensues is fierce. But all such auctions have more losers than winners.

To outwit the market colleges use a device called "opportunity hiring," which works like this: When it appears that a qualified minority faculty person at some other institution is available, however little need there may presently be for a person in that academic field, the normal process of searching and vetting will be bypassed and the appointment made by administrative fiat. Intellectually unjustified this may be — but landing a promising minority scholar, or one of good repute, is a minor triumph.

In the autumn of 2001 one such program, the "opportunity hiring plan" at the University of Nebraska, typical of such plans nationwide, was given painful scrutiny by the state legislature. To "increase diversity" the university had formally adopted a plan, in 1998, to appoint faculty "without benefit of a formal search process, to take advantage of an exceptional and usually serendipitous opportunity. . .[when] doing a search would serve no useful purpose." Departments were advised to apply to the Office of Academic Affairs to request "bridge funds" made available from a special fund that, according to the University of Nebraska associate vice-chancellor "supports the hiring of underrepresented groups."[33]

In 1997 the Nebraska state legislature imposed the mandate that the University of Nebraska be among the top 50% of peer institutions (nationally) in the employment of women and minorities by August of 2002. The reduction of its general fund appropriation was explicitly threatened if that goal were not reached. One professor of philosophy there remarked, "Like it or not, what affirmative action has turned into at Nebraska is a quota system. They [the University] won't call it that, but that is what they are doing."[34] One Nebraska state senator said this: "Women and minorities have been discriminated against in this country for years.... If we have to make it so people are given an incentive to hire a woman or minority, then I don't see anything wrong with that." This, she observed with some satisfaction, was the first time that white males have "felt what it feels like."[35] The University of Nebraska is one of many institutions engaged in the same chase.[36]

Truly able minority scholars are undermined and stigmatized by this process, as noted earlier. Prof. Stephen Carter, of the Yale Law School, applying his theory of the search for "the best black" to law school recruiting, observes that the consequences for the schools are likely to be disastrous. If race preferences are introduced into the hiring system, aiming "to hire the best potential scholars of color rather than simply the best potential scholars" the outcome will be a group of scholars who may "produce work of lower median quality than the work produced by those hired simply because they are the best potential scholars."[37] Such preferences in hiring, he continues, "carry an implicit denigration of the abilities of scholars of color, the unspoken suggestion that we cannot really compete." Law schools, he urges, ought to count their costs "including the costs to we [sic] who are their beneficiaries — the 'best blacks.'" Universities put their heads in the sand says Carter; they "choose to pretend that the costs [of racial preferences] do not exist. Unfortunately for that pleasant fantasy, they do."[38]

When universities and professional schools covertly adopt a two-track system, applying high scholarly standards for all appointments except those for non-white faculty, the premise is (Carter continues) that scholars of color would not survive under the hiring standards normally employed. This, he justly complains, is "an insult to those of us who want to try."

Such two-track systems produce the results one might expect. Since they are designed to bring into the university those who could not be appointed using the normal criteria they do just that, and there is a strong likelihood that, as Carter gently puts it, "the scholarship of those who are hired because of racial preferences will not be as good as the scholarship of those who are not." Everyone can see this, everyone knows it, yet it is rarely acknowledged. Why? "This silence [Stephen Carter concludes] can only be ascribed to a fear of attacking the shibboleth of preferences."[39]

In sum: Race preference is commonly defended in universities on the ground that it is good for those institutions. This is not true. Race preference has exceedingly bad consequences for all institutions in which it is widely practiced.

End Notes -- Chapter 8

[1]   At the University of Michigan, at the very time that substantial preferences for minority applicants to the law school and the undergraduate college were being acknowledged in legal proceedings, the University continued to publish, in each of its catalogues, this disclaimer: "The University of Michigan is committed to a policy of non-discrimination and equal opportunity for all persons regardless of race, sex, color, religion, creed, national origin or ancestry ... in employment, educational programs and activities, and admissions." Typically, its right hand knew but could not confess to the knowledge of what its left hand did.

Many references to the University of Michigan appear in these pages. Its procedures became the subject of the two most prominent Supreme Court cases in this sphere, *Gratz v. Bollinger* and *Grutter v. Bollinger*. It was long a standard bearer for the fine public universities that give race preference in admissions. No longer. A constitutional amendment in Michigan, adopted by statewide vote in 2006, now forbids preference for any person or group on the basis of race or ethnicity.

The controversy over affirmative action at The University of Michigan, heated but always civil, went on for many years. The full details of that controversy are reported in my book, *A Conflict of Principles*, published in 2014 by the University Press of Kansas. The readers of the book in hand are urged to read that one.

[2]   Illustrations abound. Two will suffice. From the year 2000: Ohio State University, one of the largest and best of our state institutions of higher learning makes no bones about its target, formulated by its President and its Provost: "[T]he short term goal ...[of Ohio State University] is to create a faculty, student and staff profile that reflects the demographic profile of the state." And from the California Master Plan for higher Education, adopted in 1988 by that state's legislature: "Each segment of California public education shall strive to approximate by the year 2000 the general ethnic, gender, economic, and regional composition of high school graduates, both in first year classes, and subsequent college and university graduating classes."

[3]   One illustration: At the University of Michigan a very desirable six-year program combining undergraduate and medical studies ("Inteflex") had very high entry standards for white applicants, but (in 1996) different and markedly lower standards for black or Hispanic applicants. There simply was no other way of enrolling the targeted number of minorities into the program.

[4]   Guidelines distributed by the administration to admissions counselors at The University of Michigan were marked in bold print: **"Confidential: For Internal Use Only."**

[5]   For a full account of the details in some institutions, see Carl Cohen, "Race, Lies, and Hopwood," *Commentary* 101, no. 6, June 1996.

[6]   At the University of Michigan, for example, applicants for undergraduate admission with the very same scores and GPAs were long rejected or admitted depending upon their race. With identical academic records minority students were accepted and majority students were rejected.

7   In very recent .years there has been much discussion of the replacement of the SAT I (an examination testing general aptitudes) with the SAT II (an examination testing achievements in specific subject matters). But there are few who would abandon examinations entirely, and those who would. generally aim to do so because, in the absence of such measures, reaching affirmative action targets requires less manipulation. The reality is that SAT scores have always been a relatively minor factor in admission, grade point averages in previous schooling being far more heavily weighed.

8   There are in fact two SATs, labeled I and II. For an account of the distinction between them see endnote 7. In most discourse reference to the SAT is meant to designate SAT I, a test of general scholastic aptitude.

9   See William G. Bowen and Frederick E. Vars. "Scholastic Aptitude Test Scores, Race, and Academic Performance in Selective Colleges and Universities", in *The Black-White Test Score Gap*, ed. by Christopher Jencks and Meredith Phillips, (Washington DC, the Brookings Institution, 1998.)

10   Article 1, Section 31 of the California Constitution (adopted by statewide referendum in 1996 as Proposition 209) reads as follows:

> The state shall not discriminate against, or grant preferential treatment to, any individual or group on the basis of race, sex, color, ethnicity, or national origin in the operation of public employment, public education, or public contracting.

This provision was added to the California constitution as a result of the passage of what was widely known as Proposition 209. the California Civil Rights Initiative, adopted by a substantial majority of the voters in a statewide referendum in 1996.

11   See: Marcia Graham Synott, *The Half-Opened Door: Discrimination and Admissions at Harvard, Yale, and Princeton, 1900-1970*, Greenwood Publishing Group, 1979.

12   See: James Traub, *City on a Hill: Testing the American Dream at City College*, describing classrooms at CCNY filled with students who could hardly write or read, and who spoke little English. A recent *New York Times* report referred wistfully to this once great institution as the City's "faded jewel."

13   Other universities went down the same path, though not so far or so fast. In the days before the passage of Proposition 209 forbidding preference, The University of California at San Diego gave the equivalent of 300 SAT points to blacks and Mexican-Americans in the name of "affirmative action." Testimony before the U.S. House of Representatives, Committee on the Judiciary. Subcommittee on the Constitution, Hearings on H.R. 1909 (The Civil Rights Act of 1997) 26 June 1997.

14   At CCNY there is an upbeat sequel to the sad story of decline. Remedial courses were largely removed from its curriculum, students needing remediation being directed to the community colleges. "We're on a new trajectory," said the President of CCNY in 2002 — but the academic credentials of those now admitted are announced only after excluding the scores of those "disadvantaged" students who are admitted separately, and who are present in all the senior colleges of the City University. See "City University's Faded Jewel Regains Luster," *The New York Times*, 2 February 2002. A professor at the City University of New York, Barry Latzer, wrote the *Times* in response: "If indeed 'City

College, the Faded Jewel of CUNY, Is Recovering Its Luster and Its Achievers," that is due almost entirely to the wise but controversial policy of excluding remedial students. Because these students have much lower SAT scores ... [this] enables City College to raise academic standards and attract better students." See: "City College's Rebirth." *The New York Times*, 5 February, 2002.

15 Increases in funding continue. Here are some of the collaborative initiatives launched during the academic year 2001/2002, at the University of Michigan "to promote education for a diverse democracy": a) Diversity and Democracy Initiatives Fund; b) The O.P. Maynard and S. 0. Karlstrom Fund inviting "proposals for faculty initiatives that prepare students for participation in a diverse democratic society,"; c) The Nancy Cantor Lecture Series on Intellectual Diversity; The 2002-2003 Campus Forum on Higher Education for Diverse Democracy, aiming to "formulate a vision of the University of Michigan as an institution with commitment to education for a diverse democracy." To oversee these efforts, a new "Faculty Committee on Education for Diverse Democracy" has been appointed, because, as a memorandum (of 8 Feb 2002) from the Senior Counselor to the Interim Vice President for Diversity explains: "Students need education in understanding their own social identities." We parody ourselves.

16 The claim that it is all temporary is repeated endlessly. An editorial in *The Detroit News* on 10 December 2001 concludes by saying that after affirmative action "help[s] minorities reach the point where they are allowed to compete on their own merit and rise as high as their individual abilities will take them, ... affirmative action can fade away." Not likely.

17 Readers who may think this an exaggerated account must experience the oppression of the affirmative action bureaucracy in college admissions and appointments. No devices are foresworn; the very name of the student corps conducting unrelenting agitation and propaganda in support of race preference is: ... By Any Means Necessary.

18 Admissions Grids prepared by the University of Michigan Law School Admissions Office, for "Caucasian Americans" and for "African Americans" for the year 1995, delivered in response to a Freedom of Information Act request in the fall of 1996. I was the author of that request.

19 For a more detailed account of this kind of measurement see: *Applied Logistic Regression*, by David W. Hosmer and Stanley Lemeshow, John Wiley and Sons, 1989.

20 All these figures are carefully documented in the findings of fact of the Federal District Court in Detroit. Civil Action No. 97-CV-75928-DT, 27 March 2001.

21 See footnote 10, above, for the text of this Article of the California constitution.

22 The admissions data appearing in the paragraphs that follow have been gathered from several authoritative sources: a) *Working Together for the Education of All Students*, California Department of Education, Sacramento, 1994; b) "Freshman Admissions at Berkeley: A Policy for the 90's and Beyond," The Academic Senate, University of California at Berkeley Division, 1991; c) "The Institutionalization of Racism at the University of California," Vincent Sarich, *Academic Questions*, winter 1991.

23 *Working Together for the Education of All Students*, California Department of Education, Sacramento, 1994.

24 "The Institutionalization of Racism at the University of California," Vincent Sarich, *Academic Questions*, Winter 1991.

25 At the University of Michigan the odds ratio, blacks to whites, for undergraduate admission in 1998 was shown to be 173 to 1. This means that whatever the chances of admission for a white student with a given set of credentials was that year, the admission chances of a black student with identical credentials were one hundred and seventy three times as great. See: *Racial Preferences in Michigan Higher Education*, by Robert Lerner and Althea K. Nagai, Center for Equal Opportunity, Washington DC, 1998.

26 See: "Another Flap at Georgetown Law," *Washington Post*, 29 August 1991

27 See: "Temple Professor Opposes Easy Grades for Blacks," *The Philadelphia Inquirer*, 25 January 1975.

28 *The Wall Street Journal* suggested in an editorial on 30 January 1997 that "a bachelor of arts degree in 1997 may not be the equal of a graduation certificate from an academic high school in 1947."

29 *The Chronicle of Higher Education*, 3 March 1995, p. A16.

30 See A. M. Thernstrom, "On the Scarcity of Black Professors," *Commentary*, vol. 90, No 1, July 1990, pp. 22-26, in which reports of the National Academy of Sciences, the National Research Council, and the American Council on Education are relied on.

31 Ibid. p. 23.

32 The pledge was formally revoked when it was learned that it could not be kept with decent standards intact.

33 Reported by Gwen Tietgen in *The Daily Nebraskan*, 14 December 2001.

34 Ibid. University Counsel Richard Wood admitted frankly that race and gender are considered plus factors in hiring faculty at the University of Nebraska.

35 Ibid.

36 Western Michigan University, in Kalamazoo, uses a different device. Equality of opportunity there is *defined* in a way that gives race preference. Announced in January of 2002 their policy reads: "Equal employment opportunity means that no individual is denied a job, or training, or a chance to be promoted in an employer's workforce because that individual belongs to a certain racial or ethnic minority group." Those "certain" groups, the only ones guaranteed protection there, are the ethnic minorities.

37 Stephen Carter, "The Best Black and Other Tales," *Reconstruction*, vol. I, no. I, winter, 1990, pp. 7-48, at p. 46.

38 Ibid.

39 Ibid.

CHAPTER 9

Race Preference is Bad for Society as a Whole

The deepest and most intractable problems of the American republic, from its earliest days, have been those arising from racial oppression, racial discrimination, and racial hatred. Americans created these divisions and hostilities; overcoming them remains our most challenging task. Progress in this difficult enterprise is greatly hindered by race preference.

Democracy presupposes equal citizens; race preference assumes inequalities and creates inequalities, thus conflicting with fundamental principles of the U. S. Constitution, and with Federal law, as earlier explained. At this point I address not the wrongness of race preference, but the *consequences* of race preference upon our country at large. Long-term racial harmony is almost universally sought; nothing is more likely to interfere with progress toward that goal than deliberate preference given to some ethnic groups at the expense of others. Race preference is a recipe for social discord and distress.

Implementing any system of preference must presuppose some institutionalized division of the races. Whoever is to be advantaged or disadvantaged -- in employment, or college admissions, or any other sphere -- the preferences can become effective only if citizens have been categorized. Ethnic preferences require ethnic labeling of citizens. Each must be identified -- by self and by others -- as a member of this ethnic category or that one. Are places to be protected for blacks or Hispanics? Beneficiaries of that protection must then learn to think of themselves as black or Hispanic, for the preferences make sense only if the ethnic categories employed have identifiable members. The underlying evil of all race preference is the sharpening of division by race, the unavoidable erection of barriers between races that prefer-ence demands.

"Black" and "white," "Hispanic" and "Asian," and the like, with all of their attending confusions and uncertainties, are everyday realities for most folks, not created by preferences. But by preferences their importance is magnified. We aim is to transcend such categories. We respect cultural differences and preserve cultural attachments, but we hold ideal a society in which ethnic categories — national origin, color, and the like -- have no role in determining rights or privileges. A col-orblind society may not soon prevail, but our body politic can be, one in which racial (even if privately honored) are allowed no official or public functions. That ideal is subverted by every ethnic preference. When corporations, universities, and government agencies expressly differentiate among their employees or applicants by their race, the categories of race are entrenched, hardened in our individual lives. This racial hardening, promoted and certified by formal race preference, has bad consequences for us all.

First comes the *separation* of racial groups. The term "segregated" we use to identify oppressive communities in which the races are kept apart by rule or law -- segregated waiting rooms, segregated buses, segregated schools, and so on. Such segregation, condemned by our Supreme Court, yields inequality unavoidably, and is intolerable in a democracy. Formal preference encourages grouping imposed by minorities upon themselves. But preference does not yield a set of rules or laws that separate; calling that outcome self-*segregation* is therefore misleading.

Neither segregation nor self-segregation, but rather the separation of the races is what preference encourages. It is a separation not enforced by laws, but arising informally from the conduct of ethnic groups in response to differential treatment. Persons obliged to think of themselves as being of this or that color in some contexts, are understandably drawn toward others similarly categorized. Reaching across racial boundaries is not forbidden by preference; but it is made awkward, somewhat uncomfortable, for blacks and whites alike.

When discriminatory racial practices were outlawed by the Congress of the United States in the Civil Rights Act of 1964, the barriers between the races began to melt. But the melting was reversed in the 1970s and 1980s. The expanding incorporation of race preferences has hardened racial barriers. The evidence of this hardening is everywhere around us. Visit the lunchroom of a local high school and see how the students now seat themselves, blacks with blacks, whites with whites, all aware of their color. Attend the orientation for entering students at a university. The first day will not have concluded before the new students have been reminded of their racial group, told of the racially oriented clubs or other organizations they are urged to join. In state universities there are public facilities now reserved exclusively for certain races. On college campuses, in public schools, on beaches and in playgrounds, racial identity has become, has been *made,* a central and separating fact about one's life.

Students and citizens have the right to gather and socialize with whom they choose, of course. Formal rules or laws imposing segregation or integration are prohibited. But there is a general understanding, unformulated, that those of any given race are in one boat, and those of some other race in another boat. The choices are freely made, but institutional pressure strongly encourages separation. And separate the races surely are. In places of residence and of study, in entertainment, and even in legislatures, race divides and separates. Preferences widely practiced magnify and solidify that separation.[1]

Although discomfited and ashamed, we might simply resign ourselves to a society in which the races choose to separate themselves. But separation is not the end of the matter. Groups separated by race become *distrustful* by race. Candor and confidence are difficult to preserve at a distance. Some things thought cannot be openly said about race preference. Misunderstanding is feared; most hold their piece. Scientific polls reveal greater opposition to race preference than public statements on the subject might cause one to suppose.[2] The reality of race preferences is obscured by referring to it as "affirmative action." Better to keep our distance and keep silent. Resentment builds.

On the campus of the University of Michigan I witnessed the following scene: The President of our University, my friend and colleague, was invited to talk informally with students of the small college within the University in which I teach. The college lounge was crowded, the floor covered by undergraduates. After a few introductory remarks the President invited questions on any topic of mutual concern. A young lady seated in front of him raised her hand immediately, was called on, and rose to speak. She was angry, and the burden of her complaint to the President was this: You promised us more black lounges, but in this residence hall we have only one black lounge, and we see that you do not keep your promises. When will you fulfill the commitment to create more black lounges? Seated on the floor not far from her were a group of white male students, one of whom did not wait to be called on to respond: More black lounges is what you want? said he in a sharp tone. Why should you have any black lounges at all? Are there white lounges? He rose to his feet, and his friends rose with him. The sparks of anger flashed. In that lounge on that occasion racial hostility was almost palpable. Had the President not been sweet tempered and adroit there might have been, on that winter afternoon, an outbreak of physical racial conflict. Such an outbreak will probably come sooner or later, on our campus or on another, if preference by race is not eliminated.[3]

When "they" are known to be seeking a greater share from the common pot, "we" must strategize to protect our share of it. What they win by special treatment will be paid for, ultimately, by us. When the goods are limited and distributed by race, their interests, the interests of that race, are necessarily in conflict with our interests, the interests of our race. If what they seek must reduce the share that we have come to expect, their interests and ours cannot be mutually supportive. Race preference inevitably breeds racial resentment. Resentment is exacerbated by the separation found comfortable on all sides. Resentment leads to mutual suspicion, to overt manifestations of the tension, and ultimately to outright racial hostility.

This downward spiral has been commonly experienced over recent decades. Between blacks and whites tensions have multiplied and mounted. Only whites can be racists, say the black racists. Only whites can be trusted, say the white racists. A recognized leader of the blacks says point blank," I don't trust white Republicans or white Democrats; I want a black party!"[4]

Hostility grows into hate. Hate talk becomes acceptable. Talk radio becomes hate radio. "Cracker" and "whitey" are words widely heard, even in formal settings. The word "nigger" is forbidden and become the subject of scholarly inquiry. The organizers of hate, both white and black, are grudgingly admired, even applauded. Sister Souljah tells her laughing audience: "If black people kill black people every day, why not take a week off and kill white people?" Boycotts are organized by race: Buy white! Buy black![5] Interest groups by race multiply; exaggerated claims for the merits of minority cultures go uncontested. Double standards by race are everywhere. Preference is the sharpest thorn; the manifest unfairness of preference results, as Senator Joseph

Lieberman put it, in "breaking the ties of civil society."[6]

Hostility between gainers and losers is part of it. Another part is the hostility among groups competing for more preference. Foundations offer grants by race.[7] Universities offer scholarships by race.[8] Blacks and Puerto Ricans battle for the turf in New York; Latinos and Asians battle for the turf in California. If the pie is going to be divided by race, we -- whoever "we" may be -- had better get organized quickly to insure that we get our share. What racial groups will next coalesce to register demands? Chinese-Americans? Japanese-Americans? Jews? If suffering past injustice be the badge of entitlement, many groups deserve preference that do not now receive it. Shall there be differing preferential schemes for the various nationality groups? Polish-Americans? Italian-Americans? For various religions? Jehovah's Witnesses? Mormons? Preferences established for any minority invite competition and animosity among minority groups. A rapidly growing Hispanic minority registers its claim for preference in medical schools for example[9] -- and thereby cuts into what blacks had thought their entitlements. Between Koreans and African-Americans the tension comes sometimes to blows.

The distribution of public goods by ethnicity is wrongheaded and counterproductive. No pattern of distribution by ethnic group can be fair. Ethnic proportionality is an unattainable ideal because the ethnic classifications are not drawn on the same dimension, so there is no scheme that ever could satisfy all the racial competitors. Moreover, if ethnically proportional distribution were achievable in principle, which it is not, its outcomes could not be stable in a world in which competition by race is fomented by preferences for some but not all.

Preference breeds hostility, but it also calls for social machinery that is almost as ugly as hate. Where preference is to be given we must be able to specify its authorized beneficiaries. The authorization absolutely requires some devices for determining who are, and who are not, members of the preferred group. Contrasting racial *colors* make this seem simple. At the racial margins, however, it becomes is a serious problem. Who is black? Who is white? Conflicting views about the nature of membership in racial groups collide. Are the races categories constructed by society but without objective reality? Or are they natural divisions of humankind? To give preference racial concepts must be rationally applied; objective and consistently applied criteria are needed to determine who deserves what those of a given race deserve, and who does not.

Criteria for racial membership are in much dispute. May one fairly claim membership in more than one race? How much "blood" of a given race is enough to justify the claim that one is of that race? Is "one drop" enough? If one parent is white and the other black, we do not quarrel if the offspring classify themselves as black. If only one grandparent is black, that too will be sufficient in the eyes of most. But what if only one great grandparent were black? An "octoroon" (according to The American College Dictionary) is "a person having one-eighth Negro ancestry; offspring of a quadroon and a white." In those unenlightened days when such matters determined one's fate, such terms were part of everyday discourse. Now we must rejuvenate them, because now again being of this race or that one may materially affect one's deserts and opportunities. The question is ugly, but to those who advocate race preference it must be put: Are octoroons now to receive preference when preference is given to blacks?

We cannot avoid such questions by leaving the matter of racial identification to the individual, allowing each to decide for himself whether he is or is not to be considered black. That response is not acceptable because, if one-eighth ancestry is not enough to justify the classification, octoroons who make the claim for preference must be consistently advised that they are not entitled to it. And if the response be that one-eighth is indeed sufficient "racial blood" (of this or that category) to permit the racial identification to be made by that individual, the question reappears at the next level: Is one-sixteenth enough? One thirty-second? There is no end to such questions. When blacks and Hispanics are entitled to a preference that many others covet, who is black? Who is Hispanic?

Distinguished American families have arisen from the union of a white slave master and his female slave; the union of Thomas Jefferson and Sally Hemmings is only the most well known of these. Are all the descendants of such unions black? If response is evaded by again resorting to self-identification, we must ask: Are all the descendants of black slaves treated as Sally Hemmings was treated entitled to choose to be considered black? Or is the option no longer available when the black ancestor is many generations back, say six or seven or more? There must be some line on one side of which there is an entitlement to preference, and on the other side of which there is not; consistent implementation of any preferential program requires that we can know where that line lies.

Consider the difficulties presented by unions between whites and Native Americans (American "Indians") common in our history. We have no word in this context analogous to "octoroon" -- but is a person, only one of whose great grandparents was a Native-American, herself a Native-American? A prominent candidate for the American presidency, Senator Elizabeth Warren, identified herself in 2017 as having a Native American forebear. She sought no advantage from this identification but was nevertheless mocked by her opponents and called, "Pocahontas." The State of Michigan guarantees a college education to all qualified Michigan Indians, because it was formally agreed in an ancient treaty that, in exchange for certain lands of which the state university took possession, all descendants of the Indians from whom the land was taken would be entitled to free tuition in that university. That is a preference of substantial significance. How do we decide who is entitled to benefit from it?

Even greater difficulties are encountered in classifying persons as "Hispanic" — one of the targeted minorities to which preference is widely given. The School Board in Jackson, Michigan, giving employment preference asks who is of "Spanish descendancy"? One Hispanic parent is probably sufficient; perhaps one Hispanic grandparent is also sufficient. So the youth whose paternal grandfather was Mr. Gomez gets the preference; but what of the youth whose name is Taylor, whose suburban upbringing has incorporated no Hispanic elements, but whose maternal grandparent was Mrs. Gomez? Is he also entitled to the preference? Genealogical equivalents of Hispanic "octoroons" are uncountable in America. Is the entitlement to preference a matter of their choice, their self-identification?

This matter is tangled further by the fact that some preferences in contemporary America are given to Hispanics of one sub-category but not another. In the American west preference may be guaranteed in some institutions for "Chicanos," referring to Mexican Americans, but not to Hispanics whose families are from Spain or Argentina. In the American east preference is often given to Puerto-Ricans, but not Hispanics from Mexico or elsewhere. And in some institutions that preference is awarded to "mainland" Puerto Ricans, i.e., those whose families have migrated to New York or the eastern U.S., but not awarded to Puerto Ricans whose families continue to reside in Puerto Rico. The mix of ancestors and the confusions of family migration make all such distinctions an absurd mess. The absurdity is created by institutionalizing preferences; it is therefore an absurdity that the advocates of preference must confront and resolve.

The difficulties suggested here are enough to demonstrate that identifying those who are, and those who are not entitled to any given preference -- in admission or in employment or in public contracting -- is bound to be controversial, and probably arbitrary. But admission to a fine university or winning a Federal contract is no trivial matter; preferences create powerful incentives to make the claim of this or that ethnicity for the purpose of winning the entitlement.

If the preference is one that can be given to a few, but not to all, some who appear to be entitled to it will be cheated by others whose claim to the name (of "Hispanic" or "African American," or "Native American") is fraudulent. Many will think they have been thus defrauded. At this point, already reached in many American communities, the award of race preferences imposes a need for rules for the determination of ethnic category.

In Germany, in the 1930s, that problem was confronted by the Nazi Party in awarding significant preferences to Aryans over non-Aryans like Gypsies and Jews. Jews played a major role in the cultural life of that country when the Nazis came to power. Many Jews had been thoroughly assimilated into German life and had converted to Christianity. Marriages of Jews and non-Jews were common, and the offspring of such unions were numerous. Never doubting that Aryans deserved preference over Jews, the Nazis found it essential to provide a set of laws, determining the ancestry required to claim the status of Aryan, and specifying who really is a Jew. They did just that, in what we now know as the "Nuremberg Laws." They were arbitrary and outrageous; but they were quite rational too, because race preference had made them indispensable. They needed to know. And we need to know. A society in which ethnic preference is formally ensconced needs its own set of Nuremberg Laws.

No matter how carefully the racial rules are formulated their implementation is not simple; difficult cases will arise. So, in Nazi Germany, as in all states giving preference, there must be a formal body authorized to apply the rules. Special situations, unusual convolutions of intermarriage and mixed ancestry, create puzzles that no set of rules can resolve without interpretation. Therefore the Nazis needed some board or committee to make the needed determinations in disputed cases. There must be an opportunity for a hearing before the Board to contest earlier judgments, at which evidence may be submitted to demonstrate that a given person is (or is not), of a given ethnicity. And such a "Board for Ethnic Identification" must in turn develop its own standards of practice in deciding marginal cases, and a body of case law in which earlier ethnic determinations can serve as precedents in resolving newly arising disputes.

This is not fantasy. Disputes of this kind have arisen with ever-greater frequency in the United States. Only some public body having the authority to apply a published set of racial rules can resolve such disputes. The needed ethnic identification must be made. We need our own Nuremberg Laws, and the boards to enforce them. Cases arise in which students who have claimed preference in gaining admission to some universities have later been brought up for hearings about the legitimacy of their ethnic claims. Municipalities in which appointments and promotions in police or fire departments are in part a function of race have faced a surge in the number of self-identifications of officers as Hispanic or black. Some requests for changes of racial status are legitimate, and some are not. We must have procedures to decide which claims are to be accepted. Rules for ethnic identification become essential.

Some Native-American tribes have only a few remaining members. Some of these tribes possess lands where rich deposits of oil have recently been found. Some tribes have received preference, in some states, in the award of licenses to operate gambling casinos. A flow of substantial wealth has come to some tribes, wealth that must be divided among identified members of the tribe. And suddenly there appear a host of persons who claim to be members of that small tribe, entitled by descent to share its wealth. Are such claims to be honored? There must be rules to decide who really is a member and who is not when some get preference and others do not.

These consequences of preference are not merely awkward; they are the products of institutionalizing formal inequalities by race. However repugnant we may find the rules to resolve racial uncertainties, they must be devised and applied where ethnic preferences have been incorporated among us. Such preferences do more than encourage racial hostilities. The force us, as the Nazis used to proclaimed with zealous bigotry, to "think with our blood."

Advocates of affirmative action often contend, not intending irony, that preferences will produce greater understanding among the races and promote their mutual harmony. The real outcome is quite the reverse. Preference yields *dis*harmony, *dis*trust, and *dis*integration.

Success in maintaining a democracy does not require that citizens be fond of one another, or be like one another. Homogeneity of religion, of culture, of background is certainly not essential, and is hardly possible in a democracy like ours. But democratic government does require that the members of the community see one another as fellow citizens, as civic equals -- equal in their opportunity to participate, equal in the protection given to all by the laws. That vision of equal citizenship is inconsistent with race preference. If ever we are to approach our common goal of racial comity and wide civic decency, all preference by race, and all promise of such preference, must end.

Race preference obliges everyone to think early and often about his race. Race becomes the background matter of every public issue, the intensifying ingredient of nearly every community controversy, the salt in nearly every social wound. Consciousness of racial identity comes to share center stage with consciousness of citizenship. Racial identification is first authorized, then promoted, then supposed and even demanded by government decree. Employers are judged suitable for government contracts and colleges are judged worthy of accreditation, in the light of their efforts to approximate racial proportionality. The ratios of ethnic distribution become the implicit standards of social justice. So employers count their employees by race, hire by race, promote by race; universities admit by race and give scholarships by race, even distribute prizes by race. Symphony orchestras categorize their players by race and audition competing candidates by race.[10] Artists exhibit their paintings by race.[11] Librarians are assigned by race.[12] Applicants for appointment to college faculties are, of course, carefully evaluated by race. We count crimes by race, and criminals by race, and the victims of crimes by race. We give honors by race, and note achievements by race.[13] Even juries must be balanced by race.[14] In every sphere those who would advance in their work must be seen (and come to see themselves), as a member of this race or that one, as black or white, as Hispanic or Native-American. All that happens in the push and pull of daily life comes to be seen through the lens of race.

But advantage and disadvantage tied to race leads inexorably to racial conflict. For our American society of many races ethnic preference is deeply corrupting. It is wrong, morally and legally, as we have seen -- but it is also very bad. Race preference is bad the for the minorities it was intended to support, bad for the institutions in which it is practiced, and bad for our society as a whole.

End Notes -- Chapter 9

1   At the University of California at Los Angeles in 2001 (and in other universities also) commencement exercises were -- by choice, by the decision of black and Latino students graduating -- held separately for the several ethnic groups. See: *Los Angeles Times*, 26 July 2001.

2   A poll conducted by *The Washington Post* in 2001 had these results: Only 5% of the randomly selected sample of American adults thought that race or ethnicity should be a factor in college admissions or hiring; 92%-- ninety-two percent! — expressed the view that admissions and hiring judgments "should be based strictly on merit and qualifications."

3   Monica Kern, Professor of Psychology at the University of Kentucky, confirms the point:"Most University of Kentucky faculty and students agree that there is a high degree of racial tension on campus. Affirmative action [i.e., race preference] instead of easing that tension, only exacerbates it by creating the mistaken impression that blacks are not capable of competing on a level playing field.... Most institutions with selective admissions, including the University of Kentucky ... admit black students who would not have been accepted if their skins were white." See "Affirmative Action Unfair in Practice," *Lexington Herald —Leader*, 6 January 2002.

4   The Rev. Jesse Jackson, quoted in *Time Magazine*, 13 December 1993.

5   *The New York Times*, 23 May 1993.

6   *The New York Times*, 1993.

7   *The New York Times*, 29 November 1994.

8   *Podberesky v. Kirwan* 38 F.3rd 147, 1994.

9   See *Chronicle of Higher Education*, 17 August 1994.

10 The Detroit Symphony Orchestra, abandoning its long established audition method in which candidates play behind a screen so that they can be heard by the judges but not seen — removed the screen in order that the number of minorities appointed be increased. See *New York Times*, 29 Nov 1994.

11 "Race-based exhibitions [wrote the *New York Times* reviewer of The National Black Fine Art Show, held New York City in February of 2002] tend to ghettoize, giving the impression that minority artists are to be judged by standards different from those of the mainstream art world....[but in this show] there is still too much mediocrity and kitsch, too much superficial imitation of outmoded styles, too much sentimental illustration, too many tchotchkes, too much pseudo-Africanism, pseudo-folk art and pseudo-primitivism." See:"From Mouse Ears to Poetic Pop", *NY Times*, 2 February 2002.

12 In Atlanta, the Fulton County library demoted eight librarians from its central branch to smaller branches to reduce the number of white employees working downtown."There are too many white managers," said a member of the library board. See:"Atlanta Libraries Face Stiff Fines for Transferring White Employees," *Fox News*, 17 January 2002.

13 When Charles Barron, newly elected New York City Council member and formerly a Black Panther, was sworn in, he announced that many portraits hanging in City Hall (including that of Thomas Jefferson) must be removed. Said he: "Sixty-five per-cent of New Yorkers are people of color. We should have a majority of pictures on the wall." See: *Newsmax.com*, 21 January 2002.

14 A federal judge in New York, David Trager, fearing an acquittal in the trial of a black defendant who stabbed an innocent Jewish passerby in Brooklyn. manipulated the selection of jurors to insure that the jury included enough Jews, one of those Jewish jurors being seated in spite of his confessed reservation about his own impartiality. The wanted verdict was obtained -- at the cost of a jury quota. The conviction was vacated in January of 2002 by the Second Circuit Court of Appeals, rightly insisting that race discrimination be eliminated from all official acts and proceedings of the State. See: "Bad Result, Good Precedent," *The Washington Times*, 15 January 2002.

EPILOGUE

The badness of which I write in the third part of this book is real. I witnessed and lamented that downward spiral at The University of Michigan where I have been a member of the philosophy faculty for more than sixty years. The damage was arrested and the spiral reversed in 2006, when the people of Michigan adopted, by an overwhelming majority, a constitutional amendment that forbids preference by the state for any person or group by reason of race, color, nationality, or sex.

Now, with race preference forbidden in Michigan, minority members of this University, faculty as well as students, know that they occupy their places as a consequence of their own merit and efforts. The races are treated equally here; causes of resentment and hostility have been eliminated. The institutional atmosphere on the Michigan campus is healthy. Race relations here, however imperfect, are no longer burdened by the call to justify pervasive unfairness.

The long battle over affirmative action at The University of Michigan is the topic of a book I published in 2014, *A Conflict of Principles* (University Press of Kansas). The details of that battle, the Supreme Court cases to which it led, the political struggle over the constitutional amendment that was its upshot – and through it all the civility and honorable spirit of Michigan faculty on all sides – are recounted there at length. I urge the readers of this book to read that one.

Race preference, as shown here and as made manifest in the Michigan experience, intensifies the damage to minorities it was aimed to support. Race preference leads inevitably, as explained in these pages, to legal, constitutional, and moral arguments about equal treatment. Race preference is both bad and wrong.

CPSIA information can be obtained
at www.ICGtesting.com
Printed in the USA
FFHW020822121118
49370144-53667FF